The Necessity of Ethical Absolutes

About the Author
and Respondent

ERWIN W. LUTZER Erwin Lutzer is a graduate of Dallas Theological Seminary (Th.M.) and Loyola University (M.A.). He is presently a candidate for the Ph.D. degree in philosophy at Loyola University. He was a professor of theology at Moody Bible Institute from 1977 to 1980, and is now Senior Pastor of Chicago's famous Moody Memorial Church. He is a member of the Evangelical Theological Society and is the author of seven books.

MARK M. HANNA Mark Hanna is professor and chairman of the department of Philosophy of Religion at Talbot Theological Seminary in La Mirada, California (since 1977). He holds the Ph.D. in philosophy from the University of Southern California, as well as M.A.'s in philosophy and theology from the same institution. He earned his B.A. in philosophy from the American University of Beirut, in Beirut, Lebanon. Dr. Hanna taught philosophy and world religions at the University of Southern California for three years before moving to California Polytechnic State University, where he chaired the departmental Division of World Religions from 1973 to 1976. He has lived, traveled, and lectured extensively in various parts of the Muslim world and is the author of *The True Path,* a volume that explains the Christian faith to Muslims. He has also written *Crucial Questions in Apologetics,* which charts a new approach to the defense of the Christian faith.

The Necessity of Ethical Absolutes

Erwin W. Lutzer

with a response by
Mark M. Hanna

ZONDERVAN PUBLISHING HOUSE
OF THE ZONDERVAN CORPORATION
GRAND RAPIDS, MICHIGAN 49506

PROBE MINISTRIES
INTERNATIONAL
DALLAS, TEXAS 75251

Copyright © 1981 by Probe Ministries International

Library of Congress Cataloging in Publication Data

Lutzer, Erwin W.
   The necessity of ethical absolutes.

   (Christian free university curriculum)
   Bibliography: p.
   1. Ethical relativism—Controversial literature. 2. Ethics.
3. Christian ethics. I. Hanna, Mark M. II. Title. III. Series.
BJ37.L74   170'.42   81-16099
ISBN 0-310-35791-8   AACR2

Scripture Scripture quotations are from the Holy Bible, New International Version, copyright © 1978 by the New York International Bible Society.

This Printing Second printing 1982

Place of Printing *Printed in the United States of America*

Permissions The author expresses appreciation to Moody Press for their permission to quote from *The Morality Gap*, one of my previous publications.

Design Cover design by Paul Lewis
Book design by Louise Bauer

What Is Probe?

Probe Ministries is a nonprofit corporation organized to provide perspective on the integration of the academic disciplines and historic Christianity. The members and associates of the Probe team are actively engaged in research as well as lecturing and interacting in thousands of university classrooms throughout the United States and Canada on topics and issues vital to the university student.

Christian Free University books should be ordered from Zondervan Publishing House (in the United Kingdom from The Paternoster Press), but further information about Probe's materials and ministries may be obtained by writing to Probe Ministries International, 12011 Coit Road, Suite 107, Dallas, Texas 75251.

Contents

Book Abstract

In the post-Watergate era, morality has become a major concern. Indeed, one's view of ethics plays perhaps the most crucial role in life, for it is in the demonstration of moral values that life's most important experiences are weighed.

An ethical system must be able to stand up to philosophical and scientific investigation, and at the same time conform to reality. The author carefully weighs four major views of ethics that have been offered by various disciplines within the relativistic camp. Analyzing them in light of the laws of logic and real-life experience, he shows that they are not relativistic at all. Rather, they are autonomous. Through a subjective decision, they replace the traditional ethic of Western culture with other moral absolutes.

The discussion then turns to an examination of traditional ethics. The author shows that the values and philosophical implications of the Judeo-Christian ethic are still worthy of consideration in a society dominated by humanistic systems.

chapter one

Searching for Ethical Solutions

The question, "Must a relativistic ethic replace an absolutist ethic?" is reviewed.

Douglas Templemore killed his child with a shot of strychnine chlorhydrate, and then called a physician to certify that the child was dead. After he had been informed of the circumstances, the perplexed Dr. Figgins notified a homicide inspector. In interviewing Mr. Templemore the inspector asked to speak to the mother, and the following conversation ensued.

"I'm afraid you are under a misapprehension," said Douglas. "The child is not hers."

"Oh . . . oh . . . well . . . is the-er-the mother here, then?"

"No," said Templemore.

"Ah . . . where is she?"

"She was taken back to the zoo yesterday."

"The zoo? Does she work there?"

"No. She lives there."

"I beg your pardon?"

11

"The mother," said Templemore, "is not a woman, properly speaking. She is a female of the species *Paranthropus erectus*."

With this revelation, Dr. Figgins then examined the dead body more closely and declared it to be a monkey, not a boy. In response, Templemore produced an affidavit that explained the "child" was produced by the artificial insemination of a female ape, named Derry, species *Paranthropus erectus* with the donor being Douglas M. Templemore.

In the ensuing exchange, Templemore insists that the inspector treat this as a murder.

"I have killed my child, Inspector."

"I've grasped that. But this . . . this creature isn't a . . . it doesn't present. . . ."

"He's been christened, Inspector, and his birth duly entered at the registry office under the name of Garry Ralph Templemore."

"Under what name was the mother entered?"

"Under her own, Inspector: 'Native woman from New Guinea, known as Derry.'"

"False declaration!" cried the inspector triumphantly. "The whole registration is invalid."

"The mother isn't a woman."

"That remains to be proved."

"Why, you yourself. . . ."

"Opinions are divided."

"Divided? Divided about what? Whose opinions?"

"Those of the leading anthropologists, about the species the *Paranthropus* belongs to. It's an intermediate species: Man or ape? It may well be that Derry is a woman after all. It's up to you to prove the contrary if you can. In the meantime her child is my son, before God and the law."

This provocative discussion and the circumstances that gave rise to it are taken from the opening scene of a novel by Vercors entitled, *You Shall Know Them*. This book describes the experiences of Douglas Templemore during a series of trials called to determine whether or not he was guilty of infanticide. Scientists, philosophers, and theologians attempt to establish a criterion for determining whether the *Paranthropus erectus* is, or is not, human.

Ethics can be properly understood only in light of the value placed upon the human species. Throughout history, differential treatment of man* and animals has been justified by an appeal to the difference in kind between the two.

In our day, the nature of the distinction between human and animal is often debated. According to evolutionary doctrine, we have come up through the animal world; hence we differ from animals in degree (e.g., humans are generally more intelligent), but not in kind (humans and animals are not fundamentally different). Behaviorism links humans with animals by insisting that both are products of either heredity or environment. The behaviorist explains that both are totally explicable in terms of matter: that is, the human being does not possess an immaterial soul or spirit.

The closer we view ourselves as linked to the animal world, the more difficult it becomes to hold out for a distinctly *human* dignity, for the traditional respect that has been given to human life. Without adequate respect for human life, moral absolutes must disintegrate. A relativistic approach is a logical result. This aim of developing a relativistic ethic does, of course, correspond with the abandonment of the distinction in kind between man and animal.

"Hardly anyone under thirty believes your view any more," a teenager tells her parents. And, in part, she speaks the truth. No one can deny that moral valuations are changing. One of the most obvious changes in moral standards has occurred in the area of human sexuality. Pornography is readily available today to almost anyone, even the very young. Contraceptives can be easily purchased, and books describe in great detail the "proper" procedures for having multiple sexual encounters. The movie industry has discovered that films banned ten years ago because they were considered obscene are now eagerly accepted and only a few churches are complaining.

---

*At various places in this book, the generic term *man* is used. This term refers to women, men, and children.

Changes are also seen in a multitude of other moral issues. In the past, moral principles were frequently instilled by calling attention to the penalty involved if the moral code were violated. We've all heard that "honesty is the best policy," yet today it is not repeated very often. Why? One reason is that many people realize that it is not always prudent to be honest (at least it may not be to their advantage financially). Frequently the crook becomes wealthy; the honest person remains poor. This causes many of us to ask, "If it doesn't pay to be honest, why bother?" That is an excellent question, and behind it is the problem of finding a criterion by which actions must be judged.

How then shall we decide whether changes in the moral climate are a sign of progress or an indication of moral regression? In other words, how can we decide which actions are morally right and which are morally wrong? Our immediate reaction might be to begin to debate the whole range of moral issues, to make a long list of such issues and discuss the pros and cons of each one. But, unfortunately, such a procedure would have little chance of success. We would soon discover that unless we have some agreement as to what kind of value system we wish to adopt, we cannot even begin to distinguish the pros from the cons.

We must be willing to set aside temporarily the question of what actions *are* right or wrong to focus on a more basic question: What *makes* an action right or wrong? If we can establish a basic moral criterion, then we might be able to reach agreement on diverse moral issues. Whether abortion, mate-swapping, euthanasia, or capital punishment are right or wrong depends on the standard, the basic norm by which actions are judged. In this book we will discuss this problem. Specifically, we are seeking to answer a basic moral question: By what yardstick ought we to judge whether an act is moral or immoral?

We may indeed wonder whether Douglas Templemore was guilty of infanticide, but an even more basic question is whether infanticide itself should be considered evil. Without some moral standard, not even such a basic question as this can be answered. The following chapters will examine the search for an ethical system that provides answers to today's complex moral problems.

chapter two

Cultural Relativism

Culture as the basis for an ethical system is examined.

Any student of culture is impressed with the ethical and aesthetic differences that exist among the peoples of the world. The clothes we wear, the houses we live in, our sense of justice, and even our understanding of family relationships are shaped in large part by culture. Again we face the question, What makes an action right or wrong? The view we will consider here says that what a given culture accepts determines the answer. Whatever a cultural group approves of becomes right; whatever the group disapproves of is wrong.

John Dewey, the influential American educator, taught that moral standards are like language in that both are the result of custom. He explained that, in the case of language, there were no antecedent principles of grammar. Language, therefore, developed from unintelligent babblings and instinctive gestures. 17

Then, as humans evolved, their speech became more complex and rules of grammar became necessary for oral communication.

Language, of course, constantly changes as new words are invented to suit fluctuating circumstances. Yet, contrary to Dewey's belief, the rules of grammar do exercise authority over us; we cannot discard them and expect to function well in society.

Of course, Dewey would maintain that it would be foolish to believe in the *intrinsic* value of the rules of grammar. Some rules may be more useful than others, but Dewey would say there is no absolute by which they can be judged. Furthermore, whether we speak German, French, or English depends simply upon custom.

In much the same way, according to Dewey and others, different forms of morality evolved in different localities: what is right in one country is condemned in another. Therefore, no fixed principles exist by which we can evaluate moral codes, since all are merely the product of cultural adaptation.

William Graham Sumner of Yale University presented what appeared to be convincing evidence of cultural relativism in his book *Folkways,* published in 1906. Since then this viewpoint has been expounded by other anthropologists, such as Melville J. Herskovits in *Cultural Relativism*.

These anthropologists agree with Dewey that culture can make anything right. It can also make anything wrong. What our conscience tells us depends solely upon our tribe or social group. Values are forged by childhood training and by the pressures brought upon us to conform to the ways of the group. In Sumner's words, "World philosophy, life policy, right, rights, and morality are all products of the folkways."[1]

Sumner drew from an intensive study of both primitive and highly developed societies to support this thesis. He contended that every question of conduct receives varying and at times opposing answers from the various cultures. Questions such as the following: Is it right to own slaves, and if so, how should they be treated? Who is a criminal and how should such persons be punished? How many wives would it

be considered "proper" for a man to have at one time? Or, conversely, how many husbands may a woman have?

Although many tribes believed it was acceptable for a man to have more than one wife, Sumner discovered that in Tibet a woman was encouraged to have several husbands. He also described how some Eskimo tribes allowed deformed babies to die of exposure, and in the Fiji Islands, aged parents were killed.

Sumner's point became clear: these diversities in mores lead to the conclusion that culture alone is the sole arbiter of moral values.

Herskovits expands on the implications of cultural relativism. He defines it as a moral theory in which "judgments are based on experience, and experience is interpreted by each individual in terms of his own enculturation."[2] He would agree with Sumner that moral standards are effective only insofar as they agree with the orientations of a given people at a given time in history. Furthermore, the "very definition of what is normal or abnormal is relative to the cultural frame of reference."[3]

According to Herskovits, cultures are flexible and so we find that mores change over a period of time. Thus the norm for acceptable conduct within a culture may change as the culture shifts its ethical base. Conceivably, a given culture may gradually come to hold that a man may no longer have more than one wife; if so, polygamy would be wrong within that group. But, at the same time and in another culture, polygamy may become acceptable. In Herskovits's view, whatever a society accepts or rejects at a certain point in time becomes the standard for morality. He believes, then, that cultural relativism is a necessary moral stance, in light of the evidence.

Whenever we evaluate different people we are forced to choose a criterion by which to judge them. But, we must always come back to the same question: Whose standards? Herskovits perceptively observes:

> The force of the enculturative experience channels our judgments. In fact, the need for a cultural relativistic point of view has become apparent because of the

realization that there is no way to play this game of making judgments across cultures except with loaded dice.[4]

In America, we find the most popular expression of cultural relativism demonstrated in the opinion poll. For example, many people assume that when 51 percent of the public believes that abortion on demand is morally acceptable, then it becomes right. Or, consider the changing consensus regarding sexual conduct. When Kinsey reported that the majority of Americans have extramarital sexual experiences, the implicit conclusion was that although such relationships were at one time immoral, they are now morally acceptable. Cultural acceptance apparently made the difference. Supreme Court Justice Oliver Wendell Holmes once said, "Truth is the majority vote of that nation that could lick all others." Cultural relativism says that truth and justice are dependent; they vacillate with the opinions of society.

Sociologist Wayne A. Leys, in *Ethics and Social Policy,* agrees with the tenets of cultural relativism and concludes:

> Hundreds of carefully checked field studies convince the anthropologist that the "heathen" are approximately as sincere as we in declaring conscience. The modern relativist, therefore, abandons the theological theory of morals. At least, he says, if God wills a single moral system, He has not let the majority of the human race in on the secret.[5]

That there are varying cultural mores is undeniable. Furthermore, agreement between cultures regarding the specifics of right conduct may be impossible to achieve, for exceptions can be found for virtually every moral judgment. However, we must ask whether the cultural facts *warrant* the moral theory drawn from them.

**Evaluating
Cultural Mores**

Studying various cultures does give us a valid appreciation for the differences that exist among the peoples of the world. We should not think that our form of hospitality or dress or our status symbols are better than those of others. Variations in such customs should be expected, and no group should judge another for such conventions. But what about other issues—such as child abuse, rape, murder, and genocide? Can we conclude that the diversity of moral codes proves that such acts can be either right or wrong?

Cultural relativism claims to be based on a scientific view of morals. But at the onset it faces this problem: By what step in reasoning is it possible to move from what *is* to what *ought to be?* Let us suppose that one culture approves of the killing of children as a form of population control; how can we be sure that this is right? That is, how do we know this action is what *ought* to be done? Cultural facts can never lead us to the ought of moral responsibility.

Here we have an inherent difficulty in any supposedly scientific theory of morals. Scientific investigation can collect cultural facts; it can also enable us to build a hydrogen bomb. But it cannot tell us whether cannibalism is morally right, nor when and if a hydrogen bomb should be detonated. Because it cannot tell us what ought to be done, such decisions must be based on something other than scientific inquiry.

For example, proponents of evolutionary ethics claim that their ethical system is based on the scientific method, yet careful consideration forces us to conclude otherwise.

Antony Flew, author of *Evolutionary Ethics,* summarizes the view: "All morals, ideas and ideals have originated in the world; and that, having thus in the past been subject to change, they will presumably in the future too, for better or for worse, continue to evolve."[6] He develops this thesis by denying that there is any supernatural authority for moral values, but at the same time he upholds the primary importance and the authority of a *value system.* For Flew, morals are "rooted in human needs and human inclinations."[7]

Flew's theory, however, does not adequately ac-

**Evolutionary
Ethics**

count for the origin, nature, and basis of morals. As to the origin of morals, Flew attempts to account for them by merely stating that they originated in this world and are constantly evolving. But where, then, did the first moral value come from? Ultimately, there must be a point where a value came from a non-value. Discounting any supernatural "first value creator," as Flew does, he is forced to attempt to derive an ought from an is. In order to be able to claim any prescriptive value (i.e., any primary importance and authority) for the morals of the evolutionary ethic, Flew must bridge the gap between is and ought by accounting for the origin of the first value.

Evolutionary ethics also has difficulty defining the nature of values. In claiming that it is important that values are by nature constantly changing and progressing, this theory of ethics is putting forth the claim that it is of value that values change. The question then becomes, Is *this* value changing?

If the answer to this question is no, then neither do values always have to change. And, therefore, despite their own thesis, evolutionary ethicists have no right to object to unchanging values (absolutes). If the value that values change is itself unchanging, this theory claims that it is an unchanging value that all values change and progress. In other words, this theory thereby allows for at least one unchanging value! Thus, evolutionary ethicists inevitably contradict themselves in their definition of the nature of values.

Concerning the basis of morals, we noted earlier that Flew describes morality as being rooted in human needs and human inclinations. He explains that humanity is significant, being that part of nature "which has become conscious, capable of love and understanding and aspiration."[8] He thus infers that love and understanding are human needs.

But, are these needs unchanging? If so, then they are an absolute basis for morality, in contradiction to the major tenet of evolutionary ethics. If, on the other hand, there are no unchanging human needs, then Flew's criteria lose their meaning. According to his thesis, we may evolve to a state where we are no

longer aware of or even capable of love and understanding. Thus, there may come a time when we
should not treat another person with respect.

This is the case with any scientifically based ethical
system: while granting the existence, indeed the presence of values, it cannot explain their origin, their
nature, or their base. Thus, such ethicists find themselves in the same dilemma as the cultural relativists,
namely, depending upon a subjective standard. The
evolutionary ethicist looks to scientific theory, just as
the cultural relativist depends upon the subjectivism
of culture. However, neither can substantiate a viable
moral criterion.

Do Actions "Become" Right?

If cultural acceptance remains the standard for right
and wrong, then one problem that arises is that we
cannot condemn, for example, Hitler's Nazi morality.
As long as one can prove that the extermination of
Jews by Hitler and his henchmen had cultural acceptance (even many German theologians at least pre-
tended to approve), then their actions become "right"
and other cultures should refrain from condemnation.

In 1979, the governing powers in Viet Nam decided to expel hundreds of thousands of people by
sending them out to sea without food and water.
Commenting on the atrocities, the foreign minister of
Singapore said,

> A poor man's alternative to the gas chambers is the
> open sea. Today it is the Chinese Vietnamese. The Cam-
> bodians have already been added to the list of people who
> are going to die. Why not Thailand tomorrow, and
> Malaysia, Singapore and others who stand in the way of
> Viet Nam's dreams?[9]

Without an absolute moral standard we might well
ask, "Why not?" If, from the point of view of those
in power, the systematic starvation and drowning of
innocent families is necessary to preserve Viet Nam's
culture, so be it. Cultural relativists cannot protest,
for in so doing, they would be appealing to a standard
derived from a source other than culture.

Herskovits appears to have anticipated this objection by differentiating between absolutes and universals. He believes that although there are no absolutes, universals do exist. Absolutes, or absolute values, are the basic criteria for judging actions. Herskovits denies that these exist. Universals, on the other hand, are for Herskovits the common denominators extracted from the various cultures. He writes, "Morality is a universal, and so is enjoyment of beauty and some standard for truth."[10]

Unfortunately, however, such a concession does not present a sufficient criterion by which to condemn wanton cruelty. No one questions whether Hitler or the Vietnamese had a theory of morality or whether they enjoyed beauty and had some standard for truth. The question is, What *kind* of morality, beauty, and truth did they accept? Without a specific criterion for determining ethical conduct, no ultimate or absolute moral judgment can be made of atrocities that have cultural acceptance.

Cultural relativism also inevitably leads to individual relativism. If there are no transcultural values, where does the group derive the authority to become the source of values? Ultimately, this authority must rest with individuals. The group, the race, or the individual becomes the standard. The individual, however, may quite logically reason that he or she need not follow the group, since there is no independent criterion for moral options.

In the final analysis do not the relativists themselves do this? Sumner's book, *Folkways,* was published in 1906 when American culture as a whole accepted absolute values. Why did not Sumner stay within the strictures of his own cultural milieu? Surely it must be because he believed that, in his case at least, the moral standard rested with his own findings rather than with the cultural group into which he was born and in which he lived.

Perhaps we can understand this inconsistency more clearly if we think of it in this way. Cultural relativism denies all moral absolutes, yet it wants to proclaim its own absolute: *culture!* But can a cultural relativist expect me to accept this ethic if my culture is opposed to this theory? The answer, of course, is no.

Suppose that 51 percent of the people in my culture (the U.S.A.) accept moral absolutes. Then cultural relativism itself becomes morally unacceptable, for if culture can make anything right, it can also make anything wrong!

Cultural relativism also leaves other questions unanswered. For example, what happens when the values of two cultures collide? What if one country believes that it is superior to all others and therefore justifies war and genocide to dominate the world? According to cultural relativism, since these are the beliefs of an entire culture, they are therefore morally right. But now other cultures must protect themselves against such aggression. Are they also morally right? If so, in what sense can such contradictory moral beliefs *both* be considered right? Is there no transcultural standard to which rational people can appeal?

Finally, if cultural relativism is correct, there would be no place for a reformer. For example, why should Martin Luther King, Jr., have provided leadership in working for equality in human rights if, as the cultural relativist contends, what the culture is presently doing must be considered morally right? According to cultural relativism, any person out of step with her or his culture is always morally wrong. In such an approach King's actions would have to be considered morally wrong, because the cultural relativist defines evil as opposing the status quo.

We can be grateful that those who opposed slavery and child labor were not cultural relativists. Many people have died for what they believed because they were convinced that their culture was wrong. History is filled with martyrs who took a stand against the prevailing custom. Most of those who have stood against their culture appealed to a higher standard than cultural acceptance when they disagreed with majority opinion.

The differences among cultures regarding morality cannot prove more than the facts warrant. Studies indicate that differences in moral codes do exist; that is the only legitimate conclusion that can be drawn by anthropologists. However, whether such differences *ought* to exist, or whether all moral viewpoints are equal, must be settled by some other means than simply collecting facts. As we have seen, cultural relativism is actually an absolutist ethical system, with culture substituted for the absolute of traditional ethics. We shall have to look elsewhere for a more satisfying answer to the question of what makes an action right or wrong.

chapter three

Situation Ethics

Joseph Fletcher's popular theory, "situation ethics," is examined. The author concludes that "love" as the foundation for an ethical system is subjective, and he considers the implications for everyday life of such a system.

At the Battle of the Bulge, a Mr. Bergmeier was captured by the Russians and held in Wales as a prisoner of war. Later, his wife was picked up by a Soviet patrol and taken to a prison in the Ukraine. When Mr. Bergmeier was released from prison, he began looking for his children. He found two of them in a detention school run by the Russians. The oldest, Hans, was found hiding in a cellar. The children had no idea where their mother was, but they joined the search, hoping to find her somewhere.

While in prison in the Ukraine, Mrs. Bergmeier learned that her husband and family were looking for her. She longed to return to them but serious illness or pregnancy were the only conditions for release. After considerable thought, she asked a German guard to have sexual relations with her, and he consented. She became pregnant, and a few months later she was sent

27

back to Berlin to join her family. Overjoyed at her return, the family welcomed her back, even though she told them how she had arranged her release. When baby Deitrich was born, they loved him because he had brought the family back together.

Did Mrs. Bergmeier do the right thing?

Joseph Fletcher, in *Situation Ethics,* uses this story to illustrate how the "new morality" should be applied.[11] According to him, three basic approaches can be used in making moral decisions and all of the ethical systems of the past can be classified according to these three categories.

Three Types of Ethical Systems

The first approach to making moral decisions, according to Fletcher, is *legalism*. He believes that with the legalistic approach,

> one enters into every decision-making situation encumbered with a whole apparatus of prefabricated rules and regulations. Not just the spirit but the letter of the law reigns. . . . Solutions are preset, and you can "look them up" in a book—a Bible or a confessor's manual.[12]

Clearly, a "legalist" in the Christian tradition would insist that Mrs. Bergmeier did evil when she had sexual relations with the guard. The seventh commandment, "You shall not commit adultery" (Exod. 20:14), would be regarded as a universal law that allows for no exceptions. (Whether the application of this commandment to this situation constitutes legalism will be explained further in chapter 8.)

Traditional Christianity has regarded the precepts of the Bible as having binding authority in all situations—even when a mother is locked in a prison and separated from her family. Legalists believe they know in advance whether a given act is right or wrong, quite apart from the context of a given situation.

Fletcher insists that such an approach is untenable. He maintains that legalism must be rejected because it is more concerned with the law than with people. He maintains that, rather than judging each situation individually, legalism even condemns those who break the commandments because of loving concern.

On the opposite end of the moral spectrum we find the advocates of *antinomianism,* Fletcher's second category. This term simply means "against law." Antinomians believe that there are no rules to follow in making ethical decisions. Individuals are thrown into a world they cannot comprehend rationally; they are caught in a universe that gives them no principles by which they can judge moral actions.

What would the antinomians say about Mrs. Bergmeier? They would see nothing wrong with her sexual relationship. In fact, in their view, the prohibition against adultery would not necessarily be valid in *any* situation. Since they reject all moral principles, antinomians have no basis for determining whether the act was moral or immoral. Furthermore, it would not really matter. The fact that she made the decision is to her credit; *what* she decided makes no difference.

Fletcher's third category, and his personal choice, is *situationism,* better known as situation ethics or the new morality. This view promises to find a middle path, for it rejects both legalism and antinomianism. The situationist rejects legalism because it puts principles ahead of people and emphasizes the letter of the law rather than love. Conversely, the situationist also accuses those who hold to antinomianism of refusing to think seriously about the demands of love, pointing out that antinomianism scorns any criterion for judging a moral act.

Situationism does not reject the moral rules of the past, but neither is it bound by them. It seeks to use the rules whenever they are useful, but it discards them if they happen to conflict with "love." Remember, love is regarded as a higher principle than law. As a situationist Fletcher would condone the action of Mrs. Bergmeier in the Russian prison camp. While in other situations such an act may be immoral, this one was moral because of the situation.

What Makes an Act Right or Wrong?

What then makes an act moral? For Fletcher the sole arbiter of morality in any situation is love. This is the first premise of situationism we will consider. Fletcher agrees with John A. T. Robinson, who writes, "If we have the heart of the matter in us, if our eye is single, then love will find the way, its own particular way, in every individual situation."[13] Therefore, no commandment can infringe on what love demands. Sex relations outside of marriage are not intrinsically wrong; the only intrinsic evil becomes the lack of love.

Fletcher never tires of quoting Romans 13:8: "Let no debt remain outstanding, except the continuing debt to love one another, for he who loves his fellow man has fulfilled the law." Similarly, Christ said, "'Love the Lord your God with all your heart and with all your soul and with all your mind. . . . Love your neighbor as yourself.' All the Law and the Prophets hang on these two commandments" (Matt. 22:37–40). For situationists, this summary becomes the only absolute. No universal rules can be derived from the universal commandment of love. Every one of the Ten Commandments is subject to exceptions. Situationists say it may be our *duty* to break any or all of them if love demands it in a certain situation.

Situationism therefore operates as a middle-of-the-road ethical theory. It repudiates legalism and antinomianism and asserts that "everything else without exception, all laws and rules and principles and ideals and norms, are only *contingent*. They are only valid *if they happen* to serve love in any situation."[14] Adultery, lying, and murder are not always wrong; in some situations they may be loving acts.

A second premise of situationism affirms that the one absolute, love, should be defined in utilitarian terms. This means that actions should be judged by whether or not they contribute to the greatest good for the greatest number.

Jeremy Bentham is generally regarded as the founder of the utilitarian movement. He came upon the principle of utility as expressed by David Hume and applied it to social and ethical problems. Briefly, the theory asserts that moral decisions can be made by calculating the pleasure and the pain that result from any act. In such calculation, each individual is treated equally; hence morality becomes democratic. A moral action is one that produces more pleasure and less pain than any substitute action. In an immoral action, the pain would outweigh the pleasure. But in order to achieve the correct balance, pleasure and pain must be measured. Only in this way can one be sure that the greatest good for the greatest number of people will prevail, or more accurately, that the amount of pleasure in the world will be greater than the amount of pain.

The practical implications of Bentham's utilitarianism are of particular interest. It is apparent that this theory has been frequently implemented, especially by some political regimes. Since Bentham was interested in the principle of utility for governmental action, let us consider Gordon Clark's concrete example of how utilitarianism operates:

> Let us suppose a nation were composed of ninety percent indigenous stock, blond Nordics, and ten per cent of a despised and hated minority—Jews, for instance. Now, the indigenous, homogeneous stock, having been reared in the rigorous, warlike, and superior virtues of primitive Teutonic barbarism, finds great pleasure, not in scalping white men with tomahawks, but in a more refined and scientific torturing of Semites. It is all good, clean fun, and very profitable, too. The execution or torture of each member of the inferior race gives pleasure to millions. Even if—the point need not be debated—even if the pain of torture is greater than the pleasure of any one of the superior Nazis, the pain cannot outweigh the sum of the pleasures of the millions. If there should be any possibility of the pain's being greater than the pleasure, the least scientific of a race of scientists could easily adjust the degree of torture; or, better, the national department of education could step-up the courses in torture-appreciation. And the greatest good of the greatest number will prevail.[15]

Fletcher acknowledges that situationism is essentially utilitarianism. Although he holds that situationism modifies the pleasure principle of utilitarianism and calls it the *agape* (love) principle, the difference between the two is merely a matter of words. "Then what remains as a difference between the Christian [situationist] and most utilitarians is only the language used, and their different answers given to the question, 'Why be concerned, why care?'—

which is once again the metaethical question."[16]
Situationism, then, judges all moral decisions by
whether or not they contribute to the greatest good for
the greatest number.*

Fletcher, along with the utilitarians, is forced to
accept the view that the end justifies the means. This
is the third major premise of situationism we will
consider. "What was once charged as an accusation
against the Jesuits is here frankly embraced: *finis
sanctificat media.*"[18]

Fletcher relates the story of how Lenin was becoming weary of being told that he had no ethics
because he used force in foreign and civil conflicts.
Some disciples of Tolstoy accused him of believing
that the end justifies the means. Finally, Lenin shot
back, "If the end does not justify the means, then in
the name of sanity and justice, *what does?*"[19]

Fletcher agrees wholeheartedly. If the end does not
justify the means, then nothing else does.

Of course, no one quarrels with the theory that the
end justifies the means, if the end and the means are
qualified. Even in moral matters, a Christian might
assert that the goal (end) of all actions ought to be the
glory of God, and the means to this end requires
obedience to His revealed will. But Fletcher's interpretation of "the end justifies the means" remains
quite different. He believes it is *right* to lie, cheat,
steal, or murder, so long as one has a valid end in
view. And, of course, as we will see later, that end is
one *chosen* (sometimes arbitrarily) by the one who
acts. Thus, dictators have often had minority groups
executed for the "good" of their country. In fact,
every imaginable form of brutality has been justified
on the basis of such reasoning.

However, situationism should not be rejected simply because it can be used to justify such things as
torture and massacre. Consequences cannot be used to
refute an ethical theory. They merely explain the
practical application of the principle. If situationism is

*It should be noted that some modern utilitarians attempt to
avoid the distinction of "the greatest good for the greatest
number." They argue for "the maximal happiness for *all* men" in
ethical decision-making.[17]

correct, the consequences will have to be accepted. While some may suspect that an ethical theory that can be used to justify genocide should be rejected, one cannot object to the theory unless it can be proved that such brutality is, ultimately, ethically wrong. For this reason, we will turn the discussion to other considerations to discover whether the situational-utilitarian coalition is tenable.

Suppose that two football teams decide to discard the rule book and play by one absolute: called *fairplay*. More specifically suppose they defined "fairplay" as the "greatest amount of happiness for the greatest number of fans." No serious-minded person would think that such a game could be played; one reason being that no one could precisely calculate the greatest amount of happiness for the greatest number. Furthermore, the summary rule of "fairplay" would give no guidance whatever in the specifics of playing the game.

The question then arises: Is the summary rule of love able to give more guidance in life than the summary rule of "fairplay" in our football illustration? Or are both equally meaningless in making decisions? We must keep in mind that Fletcher states, "For the situationist there are no rules—none at all."[20]

The basic criticism of situationism is simply this: Love, as defined by Fletcher, can give no guidance whatever in making moral decisions. The reason? Because everyone may have a different opinion of what is loving or unloving in a given situation. For example, some consider capitalism the best (that is, the most loving) socio-economic system for America; others believe that the most loving system would be communism. Some believe that the most loving sexual relationship is within marriage; others believe that sexual diversity is best. Some believe that the killing of deformed children is the most loving action; others believe that such an act violates the legitimate right to life of the helpless child. And such examples could be multiplied.

Love, then, without ethical content is meaningless.

We make "loving" decisions based upon certain values. No one is value-free and no one loves without using previous values in the choice. Love, without rules (or some universal and agreed-upon definition), cannot give any guidance in making a single moral decision. Commenting on some of Fletcher's moral judgments, Lawrence Richards writes:

> Fletcher's decision is reached by the judgment that release from unjust exploitation by adultery is preferable to continued exploitation with chastity; that abortion is preferable to risking possible ill effects on the unwed mother. Once these value judgments have been made, love can demand the appropriate decision. *But it was not on the basis of "love" that the initial judgments were made!* The judging and weighing of the factors in the situation were—*and must logically have been*—prior to the application of the principle of love.[21]

Richards is pointing out that Fletcher's views are based on his own *preconceived* value system. In Fletcher's system, love is not permitted to make a judgment in a specific situation. Consider the legalistic dictum, *"No unwanted and unintended* baby should ever be born."[22] Fletcher makes this judgment himself, apart from the context of a specific case (e.g., whether the pregnant woman is married or single, regardless of the stage of pregnancy, or whether or not the father wants the child). This shows that, for the situationist, ethical decisions are made neither by love nor in the situation. Rather, they are made by imposing legalistic prescriptions.

Since Fletcher believes that God gives His love to all people, including Marxists and atheists, they rightly fall under the situationist label. Fletcher gives the example of a Viet Cong terrorist who walks into an officers' mess hall in Saigon and detonates a bomb hidden under his coat. According to Fletcher, this example, and other illustrations like it are examples of selfless concern for others.[23] In his view, the Viet Cong terrorist did the most loving thing—given *his* system of values.

Perhaps the most publicized application of situation ethics in America was the Watergate scandal. In situationism, election tampering would be legitimate

and even necessary so long as it is done by the political party that is "best" for the people. Therefore,
breaking in to steal an opponent's campaign secrets,
and afterwards covering up the evidence, is justified
because it is the loving thing to do.

Following this line of reasoning, if Mr. Nixon's
reelection was a worthy end (and his landslide victory
proved that a majority of Americans thought that it
was), his campaign did not have to be limited by
moral rules. Nixon's committee faced a decision:
Shall we obey the law or should we do what we consider best for the majority? (Note again, the majority
thought the end was a valid one.) Therefore,
situationists ought to commend those involved in
Watergate for having the courage to dispense with the
law in order to serve love, the greatest good for the
greatest number.

Needless to say, however, the Democrats believed
Mr. Nixon's election was not the best for the nation.
The question situationism must answer is: How does
love decide such matters?

One more example will be taken from Fletcher's
writings before moving on in our critique. During
World War II, a priest bombed a Nazi freight train. In
response the Nazis used the tactic of killing twenty
prisoners a day until the guilty person surrendered.
Three days later a Communist, and fellow resistance
fighter, betrayed the priest. When asked why he had
refused to give himself up, the priest said, "There is
no other priest available and our people's souls need
my absolution for their eternal salvation."[24]

One would expect Fletcher to say that the priest
was not doing the most loving thing. But Fletcher
states: "One may accept the priest's assumptions
about salvation or not (the Communist evidently did
not), but no situationist could quarrel with his *method*
of ethical analysis and decision."[25] So, given the
priest's set of values, he was doing the most loving
thing. But the Communist thought he too was doing
the most loving thing in stopping the massacre of
innocent people. Because they could not agree on a
system of values, they did not agree on an ethical
decision. This illustration shows with horrifying clar-

ity the problem of situationism. With what scale should these relative values be weighed?

Fletcher cannot escape the fact that he has provided no solutions as to what ends are to be sought. One of his books, *Moral Responsibility,* was written to discuss the practical application of his system. He offers many private moral judgments, but he makes no attempt to provide coherent reasons for these value judgments. Once again, it becomes evident that love, cut loose from any specific value system, cannot give adequate guidance in making ethical decisions. To tell individuals to do that which is "most loving" is utterly useless. Each person comes to a situation with his or her own value system and does what seems loving, that is, right. Here, morality has been reduced to a matter of personal preference.

If ethics is a normative study—a study that tells people what they ought to do—the new morality has become a tragic failure. As Ramsey puts it, "Where everything may count for loving, then nothing can significantly count for loving."[26] There is only one difference between the rule of *fair play* in the game of football and love in the game of life: people play football for fun; they play life for keeps. Too much is at stake in moral matters to simply say, "Do the most loving thing!" Some people might take it seriously, and the parable of the football game might turn out to be a nightmare of real life.

Morality Based on Consequences

A second criticism of situationism states: If morality is based on the consequences, we have to predict these consequences if we want to know whether or not we are acting morally. Let us assume that a detailed value system could be provided. That is, suppose that all of the theological and philosophical debates of the past were finally settled, and Fletcher would be able to provide a detailed account of what ends are valuable. Situationism still could not give moral direction, because it would be impossible to predict all the consequences of a given action. In other words, one could never be sure if the means employed would achieve the desired ends.

Fletcher candidly admits, "We can't always guess the future, even though we are always being forced to try."[27] Yet, according to Fletcher, unless certain desired consequences result, the action *becomes immoral*. Fletcher must be taken at face value when he says, "Nothing is right unless it *helps* somebody."[28] In other words the point he makes is this: We must be certain that our actions will achieve the desired consequences; otherwise those actions may be wrong. The Christian must be, according to Fletcher, some sort of computerized forecaster.

A classic attempt at finding a basis for predicting consequences of moral acts (and thereby determining the acceptability of an act) has been through the establishment of a "fund of human experience."[29] This fund relies on the past experiences of mankind to determine the consequences of a given action (on human happiness). Thus, the fund claims to provide a normative base for predicting future consequences. However, such a normative "base" actually requires prior guidelines of good and bad, which themselves require a previous value system apart from the experience. Here the utilitarian (or Fletcher) cannot appeal to the consequences as a guideline, for this is nothing more than a circular argument: the guidelines for predicting consequences are in the fund, while the guidelines for the fund itself are in the consequences.

Now we see clearly the difficulty the utilitarian experiences in trying to ascribe value to a relative value system. Ultimately, to have true value, a relative value system must, by its nature, presuppose an absolute value system. This is something the utilitarian is not prepared to do.

Furthermore, imagine the difficulty of actually attempting to determine all of the long-range ramifications of an action. Yet it would be necessary to do this in order to determine the maximum happiness for the maximum number of people.

The last observation concerning utilitarians and the attempt to predict consequences is this: What is the basis for the utilitarian declaring that past experience is necessarily relevant to the present? Does the fund of human experience presuppose that consequences are uniform? Or merely probable? If it relies on probability, does this then qualify as a normative base? It cannot, at least not without again appealing to prior guidelines. And these, then, become nothing more than arbitrary absolutes. But the most troublesome feature of such an attempt would be the fact that these arbitrary absolutes would be nothing more than the subjective guesswork of the utilitarian; and, as already discussed, this view refuses to subscribe to such absolutes. And even if the utilitarian were willing, his guesswork would hardly be an adequate guide for the determination of the ethical values of, for example, an entire culture!

Accurate Calculations

A Puerto Rican woman in East Harlem made friends with a married man in order to have a child. When the minister told her she should repent, she replied, "Repent? I ain't repentin'. I asked the Lord for my boy. He's a gift from God."

Fletcher's verdict is: "She is *right.*"[30] Fletcher believes she was right to act as she had. He gives us no clue as to how he reached this verdict so confidently. There is certainly no evidence that all of the consequences were accurately calculated.

In this case the man was married. What was the outcome of this liaison insofar as his wife was concerned? Did it help their marriage? Did it ruin it? If they had children, what effect did the unfaithfulness of their father have on them? What about the spiritual and psychological effects on this man who had broken his marriage vows? These are only a few of the questions that would have to be weighed before Fletcher could say the woman's action was morally right. Apparently, he reached his verdict completely apart from the facts of the situation. Fletcher did not carefully weigh the results of the action. It seems obvious that calculating the consequences *before* making a moral decision would be even more difficult.

The impossibility of making such ethical predictions can be demonstrated by reading Bentham. He attempted to make moral decisions based on mathematical calculations. Even the simplest ethical decision is impossible in such a framework.

Suppose a man is faced with the choice of whether or not to tell a lie to his employer. If he tells the truth, he suspects (Who can know for sure!) he will be fired. If he is fired, what will the consequences of this be? He may find a better job and make more money, he may find one that pays less; it may even be that he is unable to find a job. Can he predict how far he will be able to work his way up if he finds a new job? Perhaps he will be better off in the long run if he does get fired.

But what if he tells a lie and is not fired? Other questions must then be answered. If his employer detects the lie, will he tell the other employees? How will they react? How will all of these interrelated factors balance out over an extended period?

Fletcher apparently is not concerned with calculations. He does acknowledge that "with the development of computers, all sorts of analytical ethical possibilities open up."[31] However, not only would computers have to be able to predict the future (so far, little success has come from such attempts), but some decisions would also have to be made as to what kind of a future should be sought. Fletcher theorizes: "It is possible that by learning how to assign numerical values to the factors at stake in problems of conscience, love's calculations can gain accuracy."[32] However, such calculations are as yet impossible. In the meantime, no person can ever be sure he or she is making a moral decision, and too few have access to any computer except the one inside the head! Hence, the moral life is as yet impossible.

In chapter 6 we shall return to situation ethics to demonstrate its logical inconsistency. But the critique offered in this chapter is sufficient to show that situationism remains an inadequate answer to the question of how we are to judge moral actions. Without a more clearly defined criterion, morality is reduced to a matter of personal preference.

chapter four

Behaviorism

The ethical system that draws most heavily upon a naturalistic framework is behaviorism. The presuppositions and implications of behaviorism are explored, especially the idea that genetic and environmental facts are the sole arbiters of moral values.

A cover story in *Time* magazine[33] described a current theory of behavior called sociobiology. In brief, this theory teaches that morality is rooted in our genes. That is, all forms of life exist solely to serve the purposes of the DNA code. The preservation of the person's genes, according to sociobiology, is the ultimate rationale for one's existence and behavior.

Those who hold to this view maintain that evolution has produced organisms that automatically follow a mathematical logic: these organisms, including human beings, calculate the genetic cost or benefit of helping those who bear many of the same genes. Thus all human acts—even seemingly altruistic acts such as saving a stranger from drowning—are ultimately selfish. Sociobiology therefore sees conflict between parents and children as biologically inevitable. In fact, in this view, all human actions are dependent on   41 the genetic code. Robert Trivers, a biologist at Harvard University, predicts, "Sooner or later, political science, law, economics, psychology, psychiatry and anthropology will all be branches of sociobiology."[34]

The fundamental question here is, What makes an act right or wrong? Sociobiology answers, Whatever the genes dictate.

The scope of this chapter is much broader than sociobiology. This new discipline is but one part of the theory of behaviorism. Behaviorism teaches that all of our actions are the result of either our genetic make-up or our environment. Behavioral scientists such as B. F. Skinner maintain that our actions are determined by our environment; sociobiologists teach that actions result from our genetic code. Either way, there can be no objective moral standard by which actions can be judged. Nor can one be held responsible for personal behavior; our environment or genes are to be blamed, if indeed the word *blame* can be considered appropriate.

In order to understand the rationale for behaviorism and its offspring, we must locate behaviorism in its philosophical and historical context. Its presuppositions have contributed to the widespread disrespect for human life in contemporary society. Abortion, euthanasia, and even infanticide are becoming more commonplace. This shift in thought, unthinkable even twenty years ago, results from a humanistic view of man exemplified in behavioristic theories. The implications for ethics are astounding.

Historically, behaviorism is the child of naturalism, which arose in part out of an eighteenth-century conception of a mechanistic universe and also out of some unresolved conflicts in previous theories of man. To understand the naturalistic-behavioristic world view, we need to look at a thumbnail sketch of the philosophical tensions that caused it.

Dualism

Plato believed that there are two principal substances: matter and mind (soul). To him it seemed evident that the ideas of the mind could not be merely matter. Matter is always particular and individual;

ideas can be abstract and universal. Since matter is always in a state of change and decomposition, he believed it was inferior to the mind. For Plato, then, mind was an exclusively spiritual substance.

The philosopher Descartes agreed with Plato that there are two independent substances in the universe. He asserted that matter and mind (spirit) are so diverse that they have no common properties; thus the mind cannot influence matter and matter cannot affect the mind. He held that man possesses both of these substances. According to Descartes, the body is comprised of matter; mind is a spiritual substance.

This led to what is called the mind-body problem. Philosophers asked: If mind and body cannot interact, how do we explain the fact that the mind appears to affect the body, and the body the mind? After all, we can walk across a floor rather than stand still, because we choose to follow one idea rather than another. Descartes attempted a solution to this inconsistency, but it was not widely accepted.*

Descartes also faced a second problem: He lived at a time when Newton had just discovered the law of gravity. Through observation and mathematical calculations, Newton discovered that all bodies on earth (as well as the planets themselves) are controlled by the same seemingly unbreakable laws. *All* matter is subject to these laws. No particle moves unless acted upon by physical forces, and when acted upon it always responds in accordance with these well-defined mechanistic principles. Scientists viewed the universe as a huge clock, where every molecule moves according to a predetermined framework. Thus every action causes an equal reaction, and the whole universe is an interrelated network of matter and physical forces. Determinism, the belief that all occurrences in nature are inevitable because of antecedent

---

*Descartes's answer to the mind-body problem was as follows: Although mind and body are so diverse that they cannot affect one another, they do in fact interact at the pineal gland. This theory, however, did not solve the problem of how an immaterial soul and a material body could influence one another. Descartes would have been more consistent with his own view of substances if he had denied interaction all together.

causes, was therefore widely accepted.

The issue Descartes and later Kant had to face was: If all material motion is guided by causal laws, then the human body must be subject to the same forces as a falling brick or a rotating planet. The obvious conclusion seemed to be that our physical actions are determined, that is, we have no freedom over the movements of our bodies. Although Descartes and Kant had different solutions to the problem, both asserted that the human mind (soul) is free and hence not subject to mechanical determinism. They contended that the body, however, was controlled by gravitational forces. Needless to say, there was no easy way to explain how our minds can be free but our bodies programmed by inviolable physical laws.

In summary, neither Descartes nor Kant could explain, first, how a spiritual substance (mind) could influence the body, nor, second, how the mind could be free yet the movements of the body predetermined by causal forces.

Some philosophers thought it was simpler to believe in only one substance in the universe: matter. In this framework, the mind-body problem vanishes, because what was called mind is reduced to physical and chemical reactions.[35] Thus, the entire universe (including humanity) would be nothing but an intricate, connected network of matter and physical forces. This brings us to the question: Is ethics possible in such a materialistic universe?

Naturalism

The materialistic conception of the universe we have described became known as naturalism. According to the naturalist, laws adequately account for all phenomena. Matter is believed to be the only true substance in the universe, and it is believed to have existed eternally. Therefore, matter is considered all that there is to reality. As the French philosopher La Mettrie put it, "Let us conclude boldly then, that man is a machine, and that in the whole universe there is but a single substance with various modifications."[36] For the naturalist, humans do not consist of both matter *and spirit,* for no immaterial substance exists

arrangement of molecules, we are comprised of the
same stuff as stones or camels.

Naturalism is consistent with the evolutionary view
of man. Evolutionary theory posits an unbroken chain
of development from a simple arrangement of organic
material in a single organism to the most complex
arrangement of matter: the human being. Any differences between humans and animals are simply due to
differing degrees of complexity.

One of the best-known philosophers who held to a
strictly materialistic view was Thomas Hobbes, a
seventeenth-century thinker. Although he professed
to believe in God, he nonetheless insisted that man is
comprised only of matter. He was greatly influenced
by Galileo's mechanistic approach to science. Hobbes
conceived of the universe as a gigantic machine governed by the laws of motion. All things, including
humans are either matter or motion. For Hobbes,
mind (soul) did not exist. Therefore, the brain produces only physical motion, which we call an image.
But this image is once again matter, but in a different
form.

And what about ethics? Hobbes accounted for our
ethical beliefs by teaching that whatever is the object
of our desire we call good; whatever we dislike we
call evil. In a way anticipative of Hume, Hobbes said
that personal feeling is the only criterion of good and
evil. He went on to say that we do not rise above our
passions, and we are, in fact, bound by our desires in
making choices. Morality, then, according to this
philosopher, is not a matter of personal preference.
Rather, strictly speaking, there is no morality at all.

La Mettrie, whom we have already referred to, was
a materialist of the eighteenth century. In his book,
Man a Machine, he ascribed all conscious action to
complex mechanical structures within the human
body. Thus, the brain is a thinking machine that is fed
ideas by means of sense perceptions. These ideas are
in the form of coded symbols that are stored and
classified by the cerebral apparatus. La Mettrie accepted the ramifications of his mechanistic theory of

mind, and affirmed that all human actions are pre-determined. For La Mettrie, then, freedom is an illusion.

In the nineteenth century, Thomas Huxley embraced a similar form of reductionism. He believed that just as the noise of a babbling brook is only a by-product of the rushing water, so the mind is simply a by-product of the brain. But, just as the babbling cannot influence the brook, so the mind cannot influence the brain. He maintains that the mind is an "epiphenomenon" of matter (that is, an attendant or secondary phenomenon, a spontaneous by-product of the interplay of matter in motion). He believed that thoughts are but the expression of molecular changes. "Mind is a function of matter, when that matter has attained a certain degree of organization."[37]

Whether it be the materialism of Hobbes and La Mettrie or the epiphenomenalism of Huxley, naturalism asserts that there is only one substance in the universe. This means that all particles of matter are interrelated in a causal sequence. The universe, humans included, must then be a giant computer controlled by blind physical forces. Humans are mere cogs in the machine. We cannot act upon the world, rather the world acts upon us.

What happens to morality in this kind of a universe? The answer to this question is clearly given by contemporary behaviorists, who operate on the assumptions of the materialistic-naturalistic world view.

Behaviorism

With this philosophical background, let us now return to the realm of sociobiology. One of its principal proponents, Edward O. Wilson of Harvard University, says that "ethics should be removed temporarily from the hands of the philosophers and biologicized."[38] Why? Because in the future it may be possible to have different moral strictures for males and females, old and young. All behavior will be explained genetically. Conflict between parents and children is biologically inevitable.

In this framework deceit is considered to be a crucial factor in evolution. It is not morally wrong; but simply the way the genes survive. One sociobiologist contends that extramarital sexual relationships are also normal because of our genetic make-up.

Therefore, according to the sociobiologists, we are programmed, like computers. We do whatever our genes dictate. We expect a machine to behave according to mechanical laws, and we do not hold it accountable for its actions. Why should it be different for human beings? We also are machines and behave according to blind physical and chemical laws. It may be true that we are more complex, but we are matter, nonetheless.

Whether one views it as a totally new discipline or a revival and updated statement of Social Darwinism, sociobiology will continue to make itself heard in the future. And we will no doubt face many ethical dilemmas should such a theory become widely accepted. But the more well-known type of behaviorism comes from B. F. Skinner. Skinner believes that we are primarily the product of our environment. As the title of his book, *Beyond Freedom and Dignity,* implies, we have neither freedom nor dignity. Skinner believes that the human being, as traditionally conceived (body and soul), no longer exists. He writes, "To man *qua* man we readily say good riddance."[39]

It is not necessary to explain behaviorism in detail, so long as we remember that it is built on naturalism. Whatever form naturalism may take, the implications are the same: man is a machine; all our actions are the product of forces beyond our control, and we possess no special dignity in the universe.

Evaluating Behaviorism

If behaviorism is correct, the first and most obvious implication is that there can be no human responsibility. Some behaviorists maintain that not all of our choices are predetermined, and that we do, in certain instances, have a genuine choice. But, if we are to be logically consistent, this is impossible in a naturalistic world.

For, as already argued, if matter alone exists, it is subject to blind physical and chemical laws. Our thoughts are therefore predetermined by the fortuitous interaction of various material substances. We have no more control over our thoughts than we do over the color of our hair or the chemical composition of our gastric juices. Another materialist, Pierre Cabanis, wrote: "The brain secretes thought as the liver secretes bile."[40]

Contemporary behaviorists do not quickly concede that the loss of human responsibility is a necessary corollary of their view. In stressing the complexity of our psychic states, some behaviorists occasionally speak of some form of human responsibility. But the fact remains that without the existence of a separate substance (mind, soul, or spirit), which remains to some degree independent, man is simply a cog in a mechanistic universe. Matter remains matter regardless of how it is arranged.

In a naturalistic-behavioristic world, there is no possibility that we could have acted differently: our past was inevitable and our future is fixed by mechanical law. We do not punish a brick that falls from a building, even if it kills someone. Nor do we discipline a person for having a crooked nose, or for catching the measles. Nor, therefore, should we punish someone for stealing, raping, or planting a bomb at a sporting event. These actions are also genetically based, or as Skinner would say, dependent upon our environment.

It is clear that no one lives consistently with these presuppositions. Behaviorists themselves appeal to a standard of justice when wronged—and hold others accountable for their actions. If Skinner did not get paid for his work, or if he received no royalties from sales of his books, he would soon be heard from. He would speak about his rights and hold others responsible for the mistreatment he received. Any theory that must be denied in order to live consistently is hardly satisfying.

What is more, behaviorists cannot even trust their own minds, or rather, their brains. If the brain secretes thought as the liver secretes bile, then rationality must be a by-product of certain chance combinations of chemicals.

But why should we believe that this haphazard

arrangement is in any sense correct or meaningful? That is, why should we think that the laws of logic ought to be followed? And is not what we call irrationality on an equal status with rationality if both are chance combinations of impersonal and purposeless chemical reactions? A behaviorist who does research and writes a book tacitly assumes that the thoughts presented there represent the correct yet accidental combination of chemical reactions. But in a world governed by pure chance, who can be sure?

Finally, contrary to the contention of the behaviorists, there *are* both philosophical reasons and scientific evidence to support the belief that we do possess an immaterial substance.

The philosophical argument for an immaterial substance within us dates back to Plato and is expressed by others such as Aquinas and Descartes. They maintain that our concepts cannot be material substance because concepts are universal, whereas matter is always individual. Mortimer J. Adler summarizes the argument:

> If our concepts were acts of a bodily organ such as the brain, they would exist in matter, and so would be individual. But they are universal. Hence, they do not and cannot exist in matter, and the power of conceptual thought by which we form and use concepts must be an immaterial power, i.e., one of the acts of which are not the acts of a bodily organ.[41]

To illustrate, let us use the concept *animal*. It signifies a class of objects, rather than any particular member of the class. Under this concept we include dogs, cats, cows, and a long list of other creatures. In common experience only individual things exist, but our concepts transcend the particulars of material existence. Therefore concepts cannot be particles of matter; they must exist as a nonmaterial substance.

The scientific evidence for the immateriality of the mind comes from neurosurgeons such as Wilder Penfield. On the basis of experimentation, Penfield was forced to conclude that each person consists of an immaterial substance as well as a material body. In *The Mystery of the Mind,* he concedes that although he had once sought to explain the mind solely on the basis of brain action, eventually he was led to believe that mind and brain had to be explained as two basic elements instead of one.

> Because it seems to me certain that it will always be quite impossible to explain the mind on the basis of neurological action within the brain, and because it seems to me that the mind develops and matures independently throughout an individual's life as though it were a continuing element, and because a computer (which the brain is) must be programmed and operated by an agency capable of independent understanding, I am forced to choose the proposition that our being is to be explained on the basis of two fundamental elements.[42]

This two-substance (matter and spirit) view explains why we perceive of ourselves as responsible agents; our minds, though related to our brains, need not be completely dependent on physical and chemical forces. This explanation, then, remains consistent with the Judeo-Christian world view, *and* with our daily experience.

Behaviorism, therefore, fails when it attempts to build a viable ethical theory. Its presuppositions militate against even the possibility of erecting an objective moral standard. Strictly speaking, behaviorism does not propose a theory of morality, but it results in anti-morality. Again we face the question, Is there an ethical theory that is rationally consistent and that at the same time fits the facts of human experience?

Emotive Ethics

Emotion as the sole factor in ethical decision-making is explored, as well as the philosophical implications of such a view.

In modern ethical thought an unusual answer has been given to the question, What makes an action right or wrong? The answer? Nothing is literally right or wrong; these terms are simply the expression of emotion and as such are neither true nor false. This is the school of emotive ethics.

This theory of morality originated with the famous empiricist David Hume. He believed that knowledge is limited to sense impressions. If we go beyond these, Hume says, our knowledge is unfounded. Clearly, if knowledge is limited to the phenomena observed by our physical senses, then intelligent talk about God, the soul, or morality becomes impossible. Such discussions, says Hume, belong to the realm of metaphysics, a realm that cannot be touched, felt, seen, heard, nor smelled. Thus, Hume's basic presupposition precluded any knowledge of or speculation about such matters.

51

But if knowledge is limited to sense experience, what can we know? Hume believed that all we can know are matters of fact. I can only say, "That crow is black" or "The book is on the table." Knowledge remains restricted to such observations. (Later Hume doubted whether even this knowledge was possible.)

What about a statement like "Stealing is wrong." At first glance this might look like a statement of fact; it might appear that it is the same kind of statement as, "That crow is black." But it is not. *Wrong* is not a factual observation. It cannot be seen like a color or like a book on the table. If someone tells me that a crow is black, I can look out the door to verify the statement. I can also see someone stealing, but I cannot see the moral judgment *"wrong."* We have all seen black, but no one has ever seen wrongness.

Hume's point was this: the statement "Stealing is wrong" cannot be verified empirically; thus, such an ethical judgment is meaningless. When I make such a statement I am simply expressing how I feel about it. All that I really mean is, "I don't like stealing." Hume's own illustration examined the problem of murder:

> Take any action allowed to be vicious: wilful murder, for instance. Examine it in all lights, and see if you can find that matter of fact, or real existence, which you call *vice*. In which-ever way you take it, you find only certain passions, motives, volitions and thoughts. . . . You never can find it, till you turn your reflection into your own breast, and find a sentiment of disapprobation, which arises in you, towards this action. [43]

Hume goes on to compare vice and virtue to sounds, colors, heat, and cold. These, he says, are but perceptions in the mind. Similarly, when we speak of evil or good, these remain simply expressions of our subjective feelings about what we have experienced.

What made Hume reduce morality to personal feeling? He believed that we cannot look at what happens and on that basis determine what *ought* to happen. Through empirical observation we learn that murders occur, but we cannot on that basis conclude that they ought not to occur. In other words, we can *de*scribe, but we cannot *pre*scribe. We cannot jump from a fact to a moral judgment. Therefore, the statement "Murder is wrong" is illegitimate. All that we mean by such a statement, says Hume, is, "I dislike murder."

British philosopher A. J. Ayer, in his book *Language, Truth and Logic*, gives a further exposition of Hume's moral theory. He maintains that it is impossible to have a rational dispute about morals. Like Hume, he believes that ethical statements cannot be analyzed, because they do not meet the criteria of scientific statement. That is, they are not an observation statement about the world. Notice how Ayer follows the reasoning of Hume:

> Thus if I say to someone, "You acted wrongly in stealing that money," I am not stating anything more than if I had simply said, "You stole that money." In adding that this action is wrong, I am not making any further statement about it. I am simply evincing my moral disapproval of it. . . . In every case in which one would commonly be said to be making an ethical judgment, the function of the relevant ethical word is purely "emotive."[44]

For Hume and Ayer, ethical judgments can never contradict one another, because such statements are merely expressions of individual feeling. Suppose I were to say "I like tomatoes" and you were to say, "I dislike tomatoes." We would disagree on our likes and dislikes, but no one could accuse us of making contradictory statements. There is no logical difficulty involved in saying that I like something you dislike.

Now if the statement "Stealing is wrong" means nothing more than "I dislike stealing," then you can say "Stealing is right" and we are not contradicting one another. In both cases, it remains simply a matter of preference. That is why Ayer says it is impossible to have a rational dispute about morals. Moral judgments, he writes, "are simply expressions of emotion that can be neither true nor false."[45]

Where does this leave ethics? The answer is that morality cannot even legitimately be discussed. All actions are morally neutral. I may prefer thievery to hard work; you may prefer child abuse to golf. It makes no difference. Whatever happens is neither

right nor wrong; it just happens. All value judgments
are illicit and impossible in emotive ethics. To quote
Ayer again, "What we do not and cannot argue about
is the validity of these moral principles. We merely
praise or condemn them in the light of our own feelings."[46]

**Revised
Emotivism**

A somewhat less extreme form of emotivism has
been articulated by Charles L. Stevenson. He agrees
that expressions of ethical judgment are attempts to
evoke similar attitudes in the person listening.[47]
However, he also maintains that because our attitudes
are, in the main, based on our beliefs, they can be
reasoned about. In other words, Stevenson suggests
that values are based upon the facts presupposed by
the person making the ethical judgment.[48] Therefore,
because these facts can be argued, one's values may
be subject to change, perhaps through education or
acclimation to new facts.

Stevenson's revised emotivism leaves some room
for argument and reasoning, but it fails on the same
grounds as Ayer's older emotivism. It remains a
highly subjective ethical theory, because arguing facts
and arriving at an agreeable set of presuppositions
may still produce an error in ethical judgment. This
error could be justified simply because we had agreed
upon a certain set of facts. Furthermore, this revised
theory then becomes much like the older emotivism in
that it refuses to admit to the rightness or wrongness
of an action once a set of agreed-upon facts has been
determined. This leaves us with an ethic of free
choice but without a criterion for determining the
rightness or wrongness of such choice.

Again, no one can live consistently within the
framework of emotive ethics. A man may claim that
ethical judgments are neither true nor false, but if you
lived next door to him, his life would betray his
theory. If his car were stolen, he would call the
police. If he discovered someone had set fire to his
house, he would soon make it known that such an act
ought not to be done. And, if someone molested his
wife and murdered his children, he could be expected

to have that person brought to trial. Moreover, in court, his emotive approach to ethics would be quickly set aside for a careful discussion of moral matters. Therefore, he would fervently appeal to "rightness" and "wrongness," regardless of what he had written in his latest essay for the *Philosophical Review*.

Jacques Monod, a French molecular biologist, along with two other French scientists, won the Nobel prize in 1965 for significant contributions in the field of genetics. In an interview in the *New York Times*, he indicated that he believed it was impossible to derive what *ought to be* from what *is*. He said that if there was no intention in the universe, and if we are pure accidents in evolution, then we cannot discover what ought to be. He continued, "If this is so, then we cannot derive any 'ought' from the 'is' and our system of values is free for us to choose. In fact, we must choose a system of values. We cannot live without it: We cannot live personally, we cannot deal with society."[49] What values has Monod chosen? He has drawn his values from Albert Camus, the late existentialist, whose ethical system was that of "free choice." Values then, for the emotivist, must be chosen arbitrarily, without any standard by which to judge them.

It is the unsatisfying conclusions of some ethical theories (such as Hume's emotivism) that have led some to accept irrational forms of existentialism (such as that of Camus). Existentialists acknowledge that values are needed in order to live, but they insist there are no criteria for determining those values. The only way out of the impasse is to make an irrational leap into the realm of values. Morality, then, becomes a matter of personal and arbitrary choice.

Existentialists such as Sartre and Heidegger, or nihilists such as Nietzsche and Kafka, perceive themselves as thrown into the world without any criterion of goodness or rightness. Carl F. H. Henry, the renowned Christian scholar, describes the existentialist as "caught in a universe which provides him with no principles for making choice, one which closes him up to empty subjectivity," and as such "he is free to do as he pleases to outwit the boredom of absurdity and the frustration of despair."[50]

Emotivism, then, must of necessity lead to irrationalism in ethics. Emotivists tell us that there can be no rational discussion of moral issues. But choices must be made; disputes must be settled, and mankind must somehow attempt to survive on this planet. Without ethical criteria or rational discussion, such choices must be made arbitrarily.

Emotivism can be summarized in three statements: first, it stresses that we cannot derive or assert what *ought* to be from what is; second, it assumes that since moral statements are not *factual* statements, they are meaningless; and third, it necessarily leads to an *ethics of free choice*, without offering a criterion for such choices.

An Evaluation of Emotivism

Stephen C. Pepper, in his book *Ethics*, says that Ayer's emotivism is undoubtedly the most skeptical ethical theory ever propounded. "Never before had it been maintained that ethical judgments are immune to every sort of cognitive appeal—not only to verification, evidence, probability or intuitive certainty, but even to faith and doubt."[51]

Although emotivism seems to be devastating in its arguments against the possibility of moral judgments, at least no emotivist can make the following statement: "Other ethical theories are wrong." For emotivists, such a statement means only "I don't like other ethical theories." Neither Hume nor Ayer can say that we ought to accept their views, for they claim that the word *ought* has no scientific or rational meaning. Therefore, emotivism, by its own principles, allows us to reject this theory, because it claims that all choices are morally neutral. Unless we are given some good reasons why we ought to reject another ethical theory, such as, for example, moral absolutism, we can hold to such an ethic without a protest from emotivists. Remember, moral judgments are not subject to rational discussion.

Furthermore, unless emotivists and their existential counterparts provide some rational criterion for making moral choices, they must allow moral anarchy. Their only objection to terrorist morality would be, "I don't like it." But if a Charles Manson or an Idi Amin says, "I like it," the matter may suddenly be closed to further discussion. Without a moral criterion, with an *ought,* no moral conduct can be judged. The emotivist, then, is left with no reason to judge or oppose a dictator or terrorist.

But does the thesis of emotivism in fact preclude all rational discussion of morals? When we attempt to make moral judgments are we in fact speaking irrationally? Is our concept of *ought* something imposed from within upon the world without? The answer to these questions is *no.* Here we face one of emotivism's basic philosophical flaws, namely, the assumption that the only meaningful utterances are statements of factual observation. But this presupposition itself cannot be factually verified! This premise does not itself fit into the "crow is black" model. Hume and Ayer have made an assumption that they cannot verify.

We all know that we regularly make statements about morality, statements that seem to be meaningful and are more than mere descriptions of fact. Language is capable of expressing moral judgments, and, as such, morality is open to rational discussion.

W. H. Werkmeister, in *Theories of Ethics,* illustrates this by discussing the directions on a bottle of medicine.[52] The directions read: "Apply powder freely several times daily. Superficial wounds and minor burns may be covered with a dry bandage." Obviously these directions are intended to prescribe what we *ought to do* rather than to describe what *is* the case. This does not mean, however, that such instructions are purely emotive and therefore meaningless. The instructions serve as a rational guide for action. Its meaning is *pre*scriptive rather than *de*scriptive. This, then, demonstrates what we mean when we say that language is capable of expressing moral judgment; this, in turn, makes morality something we can discuss rationally.

Furthermore, commands, and hence statements regarding morality, can be understood and followed.

Moral oughts are *not* meaningless. A father can tell his son, "Don't skate on thin ice." The boy understands this perfectly well, and obviously the father means more than simply, "I don't like it." Emotivism has placed arbitrary *limitations* on language that cannot be maintained. Morality *is* open to rational discussion, because as we have shown, prescriptive statements as well as descriptive ones can be meaningful.

Emotivism does serve as a reminder that it is difficult (if not impossible) to move from what is (the facts) to what ought to be. This, as we shall see, remains the central problem in any purely humanistic approach to ethics. But emotivists err when they say we cannot speak of moral obligation. Language *is* capable of expressing meaningful ethical and religious concepts, though there are difficulties in constructing a viable ethical standard. It is the purpose of the next chapter to explore this difficulty.

Inadequate Absolutes: The Moral Dilemma

When the basis for one's ethical system is determined subjectively, such a system is found to be inadequate.

This brief survey of ethical theories illustrates how difficult, if not impossible, it is to erect a logically consistent and satisfying system of ethics. This lack of progress in ethics seems odd in light of the unbelievable advances in other branches of human knowledge. Computers can solve complicated problems in milliseconds, men have walked on the moon and returned safely to earth. Yet we seem to be discussing the same moral issues as did Plato, with little or no evidence of progress, much less of reaching a consensus in these matters.

Why is this? Surely it is not because we lack brilliance. The inventions referred to above testify eloquently to our creative capacity. Why, then, all the difficulty in matters of ethics? Why are we beset with 59 contradictions, or at least with theories that run counter to the convictions of a high percentage of the human race? Surely our failure to establish a moral criterion needs an explanation. In what follows, I suggest two reasons why man, acting autonomously, cannot establish a valid and satisfying moral theory.

The Limitations of the Scientific Method

Careful thought leads us to conclude that religious and ethical knowledge differs from ordinary scientific investigation. The emotivists saw this distinction, but unfortunately they concluded that religious and ethical statements do not make sense. This, of course, is patently false. We can and do talk about such matters, and we understand one another remarkably well. The question is not whether religion and ethics can be spoken about; the question is, rather, How can we construct a theory of morality that establishes principles of conduct that wholly transcend the relativity of humanly defined values? An even more basic question is, Can a theory of morals be established? Unfortunately, the scientific method cannot help us answer these two questions.

We cannot begin with a finite perspective and come to a conclusion that would be universal in its application. And we cannot formulate a general theory of behavior from individual experiences. Scientific investigation can collect facts, but these pieces of information cannot tell us what we ought to do; such knowledge must be derived from a different source.

Let me give an example: How could one prove, scientifically, that murder is morally wrong? Granted that most people assume this is true, how could this be demonstrated? The only way would be to prove that certain values in life are inherent (absolute) and that murder runs contrary to these established absolutes. But how can one prove that human life is inherently valuable?

John Dewey, who believed that morality could be placed on a scientific foundation, held that there are no fixed and absolute values. He asserted that no fixed standard exists by which actions can be judged. He said that whatever standard people use, the standard itself remains

> subject to modification and revision . . . on the basis of the consequences of its operational application. . . . The superiority of one conception of justice to another is of the same order as the superiority of the metric system . . . although not of the same quality.[53]

The illustration Dewey uses here, the metric system, is actually inadequate for his purposes. In measuring lines the result remains the same whether one uses inches or centimeters. But what Dewey means is that an act can be moral according to one standard, and immoral by another. He believed that the value of an action depends upon whether it is a means to something else. That is, nothing exists that is valuable of itself alone. But, if there is no ultimate, intrinsic value in the world, why should we, for example, pursue an education rather than an addiction to alcohol? Without intrinsic values, there is no reason to make one choice rather than another.

Let us apply Dewey's thinking to the question of murder. He might want to believe that murder never has beneficial consequences, but in many countries hundreds of innocent people have been eliminated to consolidate the strength of a new regime. Furthermore, why should not a leader—even the President of the United States—be assassinated if the successor will be someone who is better for the country? In other words, without a belief in intrinsic values, virtually all actions must be condoned.

With the rise of behaviorism in this century, it would be doubly difficult to prove scientifically that murder is morally wrong. Behaviorists maintain that we are only intelligent animals and as such we possess no uniqueness. Hence, whatever we can do to animals, we can do to ourselves and to each other.

So far, the scientific method has not demonstrated the existence of a single value, much less given us guidance in the complex moral choices of life. Science is instrumental, that is, it can be used to accomplish certain ends, but those ends, or goals, are never themselves the product of scientific investigation.

Highly sophisticated medical equipment may be used to prolong the lives of ailing patients; the same technology in the hands of a dictator can be used to systematically kill the elderly, the deformed, or any potential enemy. In neither of these two cases will the *goal* be adopted on the basis of scientific research. Such investigation can never answer the question of who ought to live and who ought to die—and why. Values, and therefore morality itself, must be posited on other grounds.

The fact that Dewey adopted relativism offers proof that the scientific method fails to establish a credible ethical system. After all, if science could be applied to moral issues, we would be able to provide those norms that could give us guidance in making moral choices. Thus, the best that autonomous man can do is adopt an undefined relativism that cannot even give direction in the simple choices of life. So what happens is that people imbibe borrowed ethical principles and live with the delusion these principles are arrived at scientifically.

The Inconsistencies of Relativism

We have seen that the scientific approach used in humanistic systems of ethics leads to various forms of relativism. This is the first reason why theories of morality that presuppose the autonomy of human nature are inadequate. A second reason has to do with demonstrating that such ethical theories cannot survive rational analysis. Simply put, relativism is always self-contradictory.

This basic flow in relativism can be in three different ways. First, although relativism disclaims the existence of absolutes, it must assume the existence of an absolute by which other theories can be judged.

A university student, bent on criticizing the Judeo-Christian view of moral absolutes, wrote a paper expounding the virtues of relativism and the supposed absurdities of an absolute ethic. One sentence read, "Christianity claims to be true, but there is no absolute truth."

This is a profound claim. Now, of course, if it is true that no absolute truth exists, then several consequences follow. First, we know that this student's fifteen-page paper is something less than absolute truth. Whatever else we may say about it, it could not be the final word on ethics and morality. Of course, one may object that the student did not claim that his views were absolute. Perhaps he would freely admit that his ideas are only relatively true. But if such is the case, then his statement, "There is no absolute truth" would not be absolutely true either.

Here, then, is the dilemma: Can anyone suggest that his or her statements are relatively true unless this person assumes the existence of an absolute standard by which such views may be judged? How can anyone claim that one moral theory is better than another without tacitly admitting the existence of some absolute moral criterion? Without such a moral yardstick, we cannot distinguish between an opinion that is relatively true and one that is relatively false. In the absence of truth, anything goes!

For example, sexual permissiveness is widely viewed today as a sign of moral progress. A broad section of public opinion sees the return to a Puritan ethic as a step backward, a return to an outdated moral code. But how can we say that permissiveness represents moral progress unless we have an absolute by which to judge sexual morality? Might not sexual looseness represent moral regression? Without an absolute, we cannot make such a judgment.

All of the theories of morality discussed in this book have assumed an absolute standard, for indeed they must. Whether that absolute is culture, love, free choice, raw power, or behaviorism, every moral theory assumes that a yardstick exists by which all actions are measured. Even those theories that deny the existence of morality assume they have come to the "truth" about moral sentiments.

A second way to understand this inconsistency of relativism is to remember that it assumes there are no intrinsic values, yet it must assume that intrinsic values exist whenever it gives guidance in making a moral decision.

For example, Joseph Fletcher holds that all values and hence all acts are extrinsic; that is, their moral worth depends on the situation. He views actions such as lying, cheating, child abuse, adultery, and murder as morally neutral: only the situation makes them good or evil. Furthermore, Fletcher says, "The situationist avoids words like 'never' and 'perfect' and 'always' and 'complete' as he avoids the plague, as he avoids 'absolutely.' "[54]

Yet, situationists contradict themselves by making universal statements such as the remark by Fletcher quoted earlier, *"No unwanted and unintended* baby should ever be born."[55] Now perhaps every author should be permitted at least a few contradictions. But the issue is much more serious than this. Fletcher's remark is one of the few statements in his books that give specific direction for ethical decisions. But in giving this rule, Fletcher has had to leave the extrinsic camp of the situationists and join the legalists, who believe in universal laws!

We may also look at another even more remarkable example. When speaking about the possibility of being confused about what to do in matters of sexual conduct, Fletcher makes the incredible remark, "What counts is being honest. In some cases, decision can be mistaken. Let honesty reign then too."[56] Such a remark coming from a situationist is indeed strange—and contradictory.

Fletcher repeatedly gives his complete approval to dishonesty in his books. How can he suddenly speak of honesty as though it has intrinsic value? Dishonesty remains one of the situationist's most important tools, and Fletcher encourages it in every conceivable form. For example, if harm has been done in a sexual relationship, dishonesty becomes just as moral as honesty. In his system, there is no reason for honesty to reign.

Fletcher's unguarded lapses into the intrinsic position causes him to make these remarks that give guidance in making ethical choices. If no unwanted babies should be born and if honesty reigns, then many decisions become very easy to judge morally. But whenever situationism provides so much as one rule for ethical conduct, it contradicts its basic presupposition that values are extrinsic and not intrinsic to the moral act. That is, the situationist claims that moral acts do not possess inherent values (from within), but only *obtain* value because it is placed upon them (from without).

Earlier in this book we raised the question, What ends should be counted as loving? This can never be answered by Fletcher: If he were to answer it situationism would be demolished. And since no rules can be given for loving actions, one type of conduct cannot be recommended above another.

Fletcher cannot say, for example, that child abuse is wrong. For in saying that he would be speaking of inherent evil, apart from the situation. Even if it be argued that child abuse *always* involves suffering, we need only remember that suffering may become necessary when the greatest good for the greatest number is at stake. Since the end justifies the means, the end need only be loving. And even the immediate end need not be loving, since one end can become the means to another end, which in turn becomes the means to another, and so forth. A system of ethics that cannot *rule out* certain types of moral action must be equally tolerant of Puritanism and child abuse. It cannot even say that no one should ever be legalistic!

We can express this contradiction in still another way. Note that relativists forget that if ends and means are relative, their own point of reference must also be in flux.

Once again Fletcher exemplifies this dilemma. He repeatedly states that love is the highest good. He should be granted the privilege of choosing his basic presupposition and building his theory upon it. If Fletcher had chosen love as his *summum bonum* (greatest good) and then spelled out specific ends and means to achieve love, he would have inevitably found himself embracing the intrinsicalist position.* At least then his ethical system would have given us

---

* *intrinsicalist position.* The intrinsicalist holds to universal laws. One example would be the legalist, who believes that all ethical values are inherent: they have inherent value within themselves and do *not* depend on the situation—rather, they are always true. Again, the opposite is the extrinsicalist position, an example of which would be the situationist.

moral direction. But, Fletcher added to love the pragmatism of William James and John Dewey, both of whom believed that there is no ultimate or intrinsic good. In keeping with their view, Fletcher says, "All are agreed: the good is what works, what is expedient, what gives satisfaction."[57]

Fletcher attempts to escape the consequences of relativism by establishing one fixed absolute: love. Thus, all things are relative, but only relative in relationship to a fixed absolute. But can this be consistent? Is it possible to embrace relativism and still cling to one absolute? If truth is what works, may not the day come when love will not work any more? Many today would suggest that perhaps that day has arrived.

The conflict that exists between holding to an absolute and at the same time presenting a relative theory of morals appears clearly in Fletcher's writings. He acknowledges:

> But it is of special importance here to emphasize from the situationist's angle of vision, that *ends,* like means, are relative, that all ends and means are related to each other in a contributory hierarchy, and that *in their turn* all ends become means to some end higher than themselves.[58]

Summarizing Pragmatism/ Relativism

In the pragmatic-relativistic philosophy, both ends and means are relative. What is good today may not be good tomorrow. In the next sentence of the same paragraph, Fletcher resorts to his absolute. He says, "There is only one end, one goal, one purpose which is not relative and contingent, always an end in itself. Love."[59]

But what shall we make of the previous statement that ends are also relative? And since all ends become means to higher ends, how can Fletcher be sure that love will always be the ultimate end? Cannot love be a means to another end, which in turn is a means to another, ad infinitum? This would result in an infinite regress, which is itself an impossibility.

Dewey, of course, would say that an infinite regress is possible, though such a claim flies in the face of the laws of logic. Yet, if Fletcher's relativism rings true, why might not love itself already be an obsolete end? In fact, might not the day come when every value judgment made by Fletcher could be reversed? For example, moralists may begin to value principles more than people; legalism might replace situationism. Could Fletcher give a reasoned argument against such a change? The answer must be no, for both ends and means are relative. What is good today may be evil tomorrow.

Like the spider that tried to build its web on the moving hands of a clock, Fletcher attempts to establish a solid anchor with an ethical theory that, by definition, cannot have any unchangeable absolute. Fletcher may be granted his basic value, but when he combines this absolute with relativism, his system has a serious contradiction. Logically, if situationism, which is but one of the ethical theories that is based on relativism, is true, then it is false. For love is no longer the ultimate end.

Summary: The Ethics of Humanism

Thus far we have considered four systems of ethics that in one way or another have been self-defeating. These systems, cultural relativism, situationism, behaviorism, and emotivism, ultimately fall by their own principles. They all self-destruct. By assuming that no ethical absolute exists, they are forced to derive an arbitrary standard as their basis for ethical decision making. Thus, each of these systems qualifies as a humanistic ethical system; that is, each of them depends upon a subjective absolute determined by autonomous man.

This is the essence of humanism: autonomous man, and a naturalistic base. Man, from himself, seeks dignity apart from any other source; he views himself as the measure of all things. Man becomes, in the humanistic system, the theme of all nature and, therefore, the basis for all values. However, as Gordon Clark has perceptively pointed out, "Ethics requires normative principles that never follow from descriptive premises. Therefore, Humanism cannot prove that Humanism itself is of any value."[60]

The failure of naturalism and humanism to provide

satisfying answers to the problems of moral conduct makes the acceptance of a revealed ethic more plausible. If revelation is able to provide a consistent system of morality that corresponds to our innate moral sense, it would seem that this option should be seriously considered.

In the last two chapters of this book we will develop the proposition that biblical revelation can serve as the basis for an ethical system. We will consider Western culture's traditional ethical system, the Judeo-Christian ethic, as an alternative to the theories we have considered thus far.

chapter seven

Examining
Alternative
Absolutes

The implications of ethical absolutes are here explored. The author shows that ethical systems based upon humanistic, autonomously derived standards are inadequate; therefore the traditional Judeo-Christian ethic deserves reevaluation.

In the previous chapter, we introduced the concept of a revealed ethic. Finding no adequate foundation for ethics in humanism and its various ethical offerings, we suggested a solution might be found in such an ethic. As we examine this approach to ethics, we will see that ethics is indissolubly linked to our view of reality (metaphysics), and our theory of knowledge (epistemology).

This writer is uncomfortable with the implications of naturalism, and the closed system that must accompany it, as mentioned in chapter 4. Obviously, there can be no "revelation" if we are alone in the universe. We must content ourselves with the alternatives of humanism and naturalism, several of which we have already examined.   69

But if naturalism* is false, and if theism is true, and therefore God is responsible for all that is, then revelation is possible. And if revelation is possible, absolute standards are possible, should the Deity choose to make them known.

The Christian view is that the absolute standard for morality is God Himself, and every moral action must be judged in the light of His nature. The Bible is the ethical standard only in the sense that it is derivative from God, who alone is the standard for morality. This must be kept in mind when we appeal to the Bible in moral matters, for it was written in a different cultural situation and in a different time from our own. Only the fact that God transcends culture allows us to entertain the hope of using moral principles from the Bible in our culture. Without this we could not hope to rise above cultural relativism. But God is. And God has spoken. What God spoke in the Bible applies universally to all cultures.

The question arises as to why the Bible applies universally to all people of all cultures regardless of when or where they live. Why should this be so? The answer is both simple and profound. It is because biblical morality truly fits each and every one of us. In the Bible we are told what God is like. We are also told that man is unique among the creatures, having been made like God, in His moral image. As a result, it can readily be seen that the moral law we are to follow is not arbitrary. This moral law corresponds to the nature of God, and to our nature as well. When we obey the moral law of God we are behaving in a manner consistent with the way God made us. Sin, or disobedience to the moral law, is therefore not only an offense to God, but a violation of our own created nature.

The Bible does not present an arbitrary moral code, and it is not arbitrarily imposed upon us. However, it is regrettable that throughout history this divinely revealed moral law has at times been vengefully and deplorably applied by ecclesiastical powers. People

---

*Humanism is rooted in naturalistic presuppositions. If naturalism is false, then so is humanism.

often conformed to the externals of the law because of coercion, manifesting the vocabulary of virtue. But inside they were rebels, looking to be free of this arbitrarily imposed value system. Harsh treatment of people in the name of a moral law that bears God's name has made it easy for many to dismiss even the possibility of a divinely given morality. However, let us take care not to throw out the baby with the bath, for we have examined the leading humanistic ethical systems and found them inadequate. Let us now cautiously examine whether the traditional Judeo-Christian ethical frame can help to restore some moral stability to a chaotic world.

We begin by noting that Christianity recognizes both the Old and New Testaments as expressing the will of God for all people. Christianity therefore regards Jesus Christ as the final and most complete revelation of God; He claimed that His teaching was from the Father, and His mission was to reveal the Father's will (John 7:16; 17:4).

One could, of course, completely reject Christ's authority and perhaps even ignore His claims. But it is not consistent (unless one can live with intolerable logic) to accept part of His teaching and reject the remainder. Christ cannot be a final authority only in selected subjects and not in others. If He was not God as He claimed (John 8:58), then indeed He was a liar. And if His statements about Himself are not accurate—if He was mistaken about His own identity—then there is no valid reason to suppose that He was telling the truth in other matters.

But if He was who He claimed to be, then every word He spoke becomes significant, and His ethical precepts become *the* basis for moral judgments. It is not the purpose of this book to present a defense of these claims, though the author affirms them.[61]

Some moralists, such as Joseph Fletcher, whose ethical theory was discussed in earlier chapters, appeal to Jesus Christ as an authority, but only when Christ happens to agree with them. For example, Fletcher writes, "Modern Christians ought not to be naive enough to accept any other view of Jesus' ethic than the situational one."[62] He frequently quotes from the New Testament, emphasizing Christ's statements about love for one's neighbor. But later he must admit that Christ did not follow the utilitarian principle of situationism.

When discussing the story of the anointing at Bethany, Fletcher observes that Christ chose the way of uncalculating and unenlightened love. Since Christ did not accept the situationist's decision (which is, for Fletcher, seeking "the greatest good for the greatest number"—by selling the perfume and giving the money to the poor), Fletcher concludes that "if we take the story as it stands, Jesus was *wrong* and the disciples were right."[63]

Fletcher's conclusion raises a major question: Can we pick and choose among the statements of Christ, accepting some and rejecting others? If Christ was mistaken when He approved of Mary's anointing of Him, no amount of reasoning could show why His other teachings are correct. To accept part of Christ's teaching as authoritative and other parts as wrong is to reject the basic notion that Christ came to reveal the Father and to give accurate information regarding His will. Essentially, when we pick and choose among Christ's words, accepting some and discarding others—we thereby write our own biography of Jesus. In this situation authority rests squarely upon our own shoulders. We are deciding when Christ was speaking for God and when He was not.

It remains the prerogative of every individual to reject the teachings of Christ. It is possible to take the position that He was self-deceived or a liar. Or one may respond by saying that Christ (like an ordinary man) was sometimes wrong and sometimes right; hence we are free to select the part that suits our fancy. But such a conclusion misses the point. If Christ was only a man, there is no reason at all to suggest that we *ought* to follow His teaching in any area, no reason to recommend Christ over Aristotle or Plato. Even more serious, if Christ did not speak the truth in all matters, His claims about Himself vanish like the idle babbling of a lunatic bent on deceiving the world. Unlike Plato and Aristotle, He could not afford to be wrong—even once.

Joseph Fletcher's inconsistent use of Christ as a moral authority became clear during a debate with John Warwick Montgomery, a leading evangelical spokseman. Fletcher, when forced to be consistent, admitted that in his opinion, "Jesus was a simple Jewish peasant. He had no more philosophical sophistication than a guinea pig, and I don't turn to Jesus for philosophical sophistication."[64] Such a remark should not be too surprising, despite Fletcher's frequently favorable remarks about Christ.

If we accept the authority of Christ at all, consistency demands that we accept everything that He said as trustworthy. He believed the Old Testament to be the revealed will of God (Matt. 5:17-19; John 10:35). Thus in the teaching of both the Old and New Testaments we have authoritative guidance in matters of moral conduct.

If the content of God's moral revelation is spelled out in Scripture, the question arises, Why did God choose *these* commandments?

We shall see in the final chapter that God's moral revelation is an expression of His own nature. But here we wish to emphasize that God has a certain purpose He wishes to achieve and part of His plans include instructions for mankind. In other words, He uses His revelation and even the struggle between good and evil to accomplish His purposes.

Earlier we stressed that we cannot build an ethical system that distinguishes right from wrong purely on the basis of consequences. If man cannot build an ethic which is calculating and designed to achieve certain consequences, can God? The answer is yes.

One remark in Fletcher's book is in full agreement with biblical ethics. In defending the view that the end justifies the means, Fletcher reminds us that the problem of evil has often been resolved by the theory that God uses evil to bring about some greater purpose. He concludes, "Here is a theodicy based squarely on the view that the end justifies the means."[65] Christian theologians have maintained for centuries that as sovereign ruler, God has the right to do as He wishes to bring about His desired results. Possibly the strongest assertion of such a doctrine in the Bible is, "The LORD works out everything for his own ends—even the wicked for a day of disaster" (Prov. 16:4). Can one conceive of God creating the world for no purpose whatever? Did He create us without any predetermined end in view? Is evil simply an intruder over which He had no control, or is there a purpose in it too?

A further illustration of God's providence can be found in the story of Joseph, one of the ancient Hebrew patriarchs. "But Joseph said to them, 'Don't be afraid. Am I in the place of God? You intended to harm me, but God intended it for good to accomplish what is now being done, the saving of many lives'" (Gen. 50:19–20). Joseph attained great heights as a ruler in Egypt and through his power was able to sustain his entire family through a famine. He did this in spite of an earlier treacherous action dealt him by his brothers.

Scripture consistently teaches that God is the sovereign ruler who can do what He wishes in the universe and among the inhabitants of the earth. He can use any means available to achieve a desired end, so long as it is consistent with His character (this is a self-imposed limitation). Suppose He has one goal in mind—His own glory, for instance. Such an end would not be immoral. God has no one to whom He is subject. Our moral flaw is never more clearly seen than in our human response to such a statement. We exclaim: "It sounds so undemocratic!" But no law exists outside of God to which He must bow. For Him, the end does justify the means.

And, of course, one of the means He may use to accomplish His purpose is to give us specific instructions concerning moral conduct. These universal, absolute moral laws should be kept at all times, regardless of the circumstances. Thus it becomes our responsibility to obey, and when we do, God controls the consequences. Since He is sovereign, He can turn even the most undesirable results into a greater good. He does this so deftly that even the wrath of men ends up praising Him.

As has already been argued, man cannot play the

part of God. Humanists believe the transcendent God is dead or irrelevant and that we must replace Him. The results are disastrous. God alone knows all the facts, sets all the goals, and determines all morality. Nowhere in Scripture do we read that His *principles* are to be replaced by human calculation. He allows us to play the game; He does not allow us to make the rules. Modern man, loosed from restrictions, wishes to be like the Almighty. We want to determine what is valuable and what is not; we would snatch from God the throne and the scepter. We want to be like the Most High, subject to no one. But can we calculate the eternal results or the rightness of our actions? We cannot predict even the next five minutes, much less the future; therefore, a book on ethics must come from God, who knows the end from the beginning and who fashions His ethic consistently in congruence with His own perfect nature and character.

In the Bible, God has revealed certain moral pre-
cepts that define morality. Two general observations should be made. First, biblical morality consists of more than external obedience to a moral code. Outward obedience must originate from an acceptable inner attitude. The New Testament elevates the commandment, "You shall not murder," to the level of inner motivation; indeed, Christ says that if we hate another person we are guilty of murder in our heart.

Second, we are therefore judged by our intentions in a given action, rather than by the consequences of our action. For example, if you were invited to the home of friends for dinner and were unintentionally served soup that contained harmful bacteria, and then died as a result, your hostess would not be guilty of murder. Since biblical morality is not determined by consequences, the disastrous results would not make this unintentional mistake immoral. However, if it was her intention to poison you, in God's eyes the hostess would be guilty of murder, even if a jury acquitted her, or even if you happened to survive the ordeal.

In the twelfth century the philosopher-theologian Peter Abelard put forth the idea that morality was dependent on the intention of the agent. He wrote, "Wherever actions are restricted by some precept or prohibition, these refer rather to will and consent than to the deeds themselves."[66] He held that if a person acts in ignorance, even adultery and murder may be committed without sinning. He concluded that those who persecuted Christ and ultimately killed Him should not be condemned for their deeds. In fact, he says their sin would have been greater if they would have allowed Christ and others whom they persecuted to go free.

Abelard was quite right that a good intention *may* justify a moral act. He erred, however, in not defining what counts for a good intention. Thus, he considered even grossly immoral acts as moral because "good" intentions lay behind them. "I meant well" is a praiseworthy attitude, but not sufficient for a moral base.

Our actions are judged by our intentions, but a good intention is one that retains harmony with biblical commands, i.e., law. That is, the most prominent intention should be to keep God's laws, His commands.

Since those who crucified Christ had intentions that were contrary to Scripture (such as murdering a man without a fair trial, bringing false witnesses, and rejecting the evidence for Christ's deity), they were guilty even if they *thought* they were doing right. Contrary to Abelard, those who crucified Christ committed sin, despite their good intentions. For this reason Christ prayed, "Father, forgive them, for they do not know what they are doing" (Luke 23:34). Likewise, those who have killed Christians (or Jews) and think they are doing the will of God, will not be guiltless (John 16:2).

Biblical morality specifies the content of acceptable motivation. What the Almighty sees in the heart must be in harmony with His revealed precepts. External obedience alone cannot make an act acceptable to God.

The young ruler who came to Christ (Luke 18:

18–29) was immoral, even though he tried to keep the law outwardly. Inwardly he was covetous, and this violates a clear command. The young man claimed to have kept all the laws of the Old Testament. It was right that he keep the commandments, but only when his *motives* also were right would his action be acceptable to God. For that reason Christ told him he needed one thing more, to sell all his possessions, of which there were many, and distribute them to the poor. The rich young man turned away; his obedience had been only external, his inner attitudes were not acceptable to God.

The ethical standards of the Bible are so lofty and unattainable (Rom. 3:11, 23), that we need divine help. Therefore, Christ promised the power to live righteously to those who depended upon Him. Furthermore, since Christ met God's standards of perfection and sacrificed His own life in order to satisfy God's requirements (Rom. 5:8), each individual must put his or her faith in Him in order to obtain a right standing before God (Rom. 3:22).

Reexamining
Traditional
Ethics

*Western culture's traditional ethical system, inherited
from the Judeo-Christian heritage, is seen to be not only
adequate, but also the only system that provides logical and
practical answers to the dilemmas of life.*

In most cases, an inadequate understanding of biblical ethics is due to the failure to grasp this ethic in its
wholeness. Mere knowledge of particular Bible
verses is inadequate as a reliable ethic. When we see
the larger picture, we have a framework that guides us
in particular instances of moral conduct. For example,
the Bible does not speak to the matter of euthanasia
(unless one includes it under the more comprehensive
topic of murder), a moral issue that has come into
sharp focus largely because of the advances of modern medicine. But when we understand the total
framework of biblical revelation and its stress on the
value of human life, we realize that ample guidelines
are available to help us face such contemporary issues.

In this chapter, basic theological and philosophical
assumptions that are foundational to biblical ethics

will be presented. Although there will be no extended discussion of specific moral issues, several examples will illustrate how the basic presuppositions would apply in concrete instances.

1. God's Moral Revelation Is Based on His Nature

God is the one who is self-existent. To Moses He said, "I am who I am" (Exod. 3:14). The Scriptures affirm that God is holy; that is, He is separate from everything else that exists. He is free of all imperfection and limitations. As such, He is His own standard. No moral rule exists outside of God to which He must be subject. No independent standard of goodness exists by which God can be measured.

Sin is the outworking of a distorted view of God's essence; it is falling short of His perfection, a word, thought, or deed contrary to His character (Rom. 3:23).

When God gave us His revelation concerning morality, His precepts were not arbitrary; they were not selected at random. The moral law is basically a *reflection* of God's own character, hence in Scripture He exhorts, "Be holy, because I am holy" (1 Peter 1:16). God could not have created a universe in which it would have been morally right to have other gods before Him, or where it would be morally acceptable to bear false witness, for He Himself cannot lie (Titus 1:2). We see, then, that *truthfulness is rooted in the nature of God.*

It is possible that precepts such as the religious ordinances in the Old Testament are not arbitrary, despite what popular wisdom says about this matter. God could have commanded Joshua to select six men rather than twelve to carry the stones that formed the monument to Israel's crossing of the Jordan into the promised land (Josh. 3–4). He could also have made the details of the Levitical laws other than what we read in Scripture. But even in such minute instructions, God was revealing His character.

Of course, civil and ceremonial laws, including those of the Old Testament, are subject to change. Yet, we must recognize that God had a good and sufficient reason to give the instructions that He did. Biblical morality is rooted in the character of God.

Reexamining Traditional Ethics

The theory of evolution assumes that an unbreakable link exists between the lower forms of life and humans. The theory claims that man differs from the lower primates in *degree,* not in *kind.* Supposedly, he is more intelligent than the ape, but fundamentally the same. According to this view, the chief difference between man and ape is the size and neurological complexity of the brain.

2. Man Is Not an Animal, but a Unique Moral Being

Several consequences of this view are: (1) Human life need not be afforded the respect it has received within the context of the Judeo-Christian tradition. (2) Consequently, abortion, infanticide, and euthanasia may be accepted, because human life is *not* inherently sacred. We can judge, then, as we do with animals, whether a given human life is, in our opinion, worth living. (3) Finally, without traditional moral absolutes, the law of the jungle will prevail: majority opinion and sheer power become the only practical criteria for distinguishing right from wrong.

In sharp contrast, the Bible presents man as qualitatively different from the animal world. We alone were created in the image of God, which affirms at the very least that we possess: (1) personality: that is, we have the capacity for self-reflection; (2) the ability to reason: we can think conceptually and abstractly; (3) moral capacity: we can understand distinctions between good and evil; and (4) the capacity to be rightly related to God. Man is indeed unique.

Some of the implications of this uniqueness are readily apparent. First, we are responsible for our actions. If a man commits murder, it is not necessarily because of a physical or chemical chain reaction in his brain over which he had no control (though we must recognize certain chemical abnormalities may cause such acts). In most cases a person commits a crime because he or she *chooses* to do it, and the person could therefore choose *not* to do it.

Second, human life is sacred. We have no right to manipulate another person, nor can we choose which human beings should be put to death. To argue that there exists a quality of human life not worth living is to play God. Human life, once begun, cannot be terminated simply because it is referred to as "fetus" rather than "baby." Nor can we use the subtle, though misleading, phrase, "death with dignity," to put the terminally ill or the aged to death. *All* human life is a sacred trust.

3. These Moral Principles Have Historical Continuity

If God's moral revelation is rooted in His nature, it is clear that revelatory principles will transcend dispensational distinctions.

The New Testament teaches that we are not under the Law (2 Cor. 3). Christians believe that today we are under the law of Christ, the New Testament, with its detailed moral revelation and commandments. But, of course, there are numerous similarities to the Old Testament law. In fact, the New Testament is in large part a deepening of what was already revealed in the Old Testament economy. Thus, although specific commands may change from one era to another, the principles remain constant.

For example, the Mosaic sacrificial ritual laid down in Old Testament law was done away with at the coming of Christ. But the basic principle that there can be no forgiveness without sacrifice remains true, for the very character of God as revealed in the Bible demands such a principle. Specific commands may change, but the principles do not.

The most well-attested interpretation of the Sermon on the Mount is the one that understands those words of Christ to be a deepening of the revelation of the Old Testament rather than a replacement of it. Six times in this passage (Matt. 5–7) Christ said, "You have heard that it was said . . . , but I say to you." He is here either referring to incorrect rabbinical traditions or quoting the Old Testament for the purpose of correcting a misinterpretation of the passage.

Perhaps the most controversial of these six statements by Jesus is the following: "You have heard that it was said, 'Eye for eye, and tooth for tooth.' But I tell you, Do not resist an evil person. If someone strikes you on the right cheek, turn to him the other also" (Matt. 5:38–39). Conscientious objectors to military service argue that Christ *replaced* the Old Testament law on this point; hence no Christian should ever go to war or resist someone who is evil by the use of force. However, it is unlikely that Christ is here overturning the Old Testament principle of resistance. It is more likely that He is referring to the practice, common amongst the Pharisees of that time, of personal retaliation for wrongs suffered. The Old Testament law was designed to teach that the punishment should suit the crime, but it did not allow for personal vindictiveness. In the Sermon on the Mount Christ is speaking about our attitudes in personal relationships rather than enunciating a new governmental system.

This discussion of one of the moral precepts established by Christ shows us that in our study of biblical ethics we should always look for underlying principles. This will enable us to see the harmony of God's revelation principles.

4. God's Moral Revelation Has Intrinsic Value

Since God is His own standard, His moral precepts do not have validity apart from Him. But, His moral revelation does have intrinsic validity in relation to us. When we violate God's standard, there are always built-in consequences.

Each one of us is acquainted with at least two different kinds of laws. For example, city hall has the authority to order that a stop sign be placed at a given intersection. Later a motion may be passed that it be removed. We can legislate such civil laws. They are changeable.

But there are other laws that are beyond our control. For example, we cannot change the law of gravity, regardless of how inconvenient it becomes. Nor can we alter the laws of chemistry: We can only *discover* such laws. Similarly, the moral laws of God cannot be altered. We cannot obliterate God's standards just because 51 percent of the people favor a change in moral codes. The only difference between physical laws and moral laws is that the consequences of ignoring physical laws are immediately apparent: In the case of moral laws the consequences are just as certain, though often delayed.

For all of us, socially and individually, disobedience to God's standards will have repercussions, both now and for eternity. We can never recover the time spent pursuing our own will rather than God's will, nor can we undo the effects of immoral acts. In fact, the consequences of breaking God's laws are so consistent that God in His justice could not even forgive us unless someone else were to accept the penalty for our disobedience. Hence, we can be acquitted only because of Christ's sacrificial death (2 Cor. 5:21).

5. In the Scriptures, Law and Love Are Harmonized

As noted in chapter 7, situationism teaches that law and love are often at variance. According to Joseph Fletcher, we cannot always do the loving thing if we are acting according to certain laws. To obey the law means that we are often cruel; whereas if we were to break the law we would then be free to be loving.

But with biblical absolutes we are never faced with the choice of either obeying God or doing what is most loving. The most loving act is one that obeys the revealed will of God.

Romans 13:8, the verse Fletcher frequently quotes, shows clearly that love does not replace law; indeed, love *fulfills* the law. Love fulfills the law in that it is always in accord with God's revealed will. In fact, the content of love turns out to be specific commandments. For example:

> Let no debt remain outstanding, except the continuing debt to love one another, for he who loves his fellow man has fulfilled the law. The commandments, "Do not commit adultery," "Do not murder," "Do not steal," "Do not covet," and whatever other commandment there may be, are summed up in this one rule: "Love your neighbor as yourself." Love does no harm to its neighbor. Therefore love is the fulfillment of the law. (Rom. 13:8–10)

No one in history has ever improved on these ethical principles. They bring peace and harmony wherever they are practiced.

Another passage in the New Testament gives perhaps the clearest teaching concerning the fact that in the Bible love and law are not at variance: "And this is love: that we walk in obedience to His commands" (2 John 6). Jesus repeatedly said that if we love Him we will keep His commandments (John 14:15). Thus, God's revealed moral law is the expression of His love: it defines specifically what His love requires.

6. Obedience to God's Laws Is Not Legalism

A frequent objection to biblical morality is that it places us under a legalistic code. We immediately think of those who dutifully carry out trivial religious requirements, and who cannot enjoy even the innocent pleasures of life. There are two things that can be said in response to this complaint. First, it is possible to apply biblical morality *without being legalistic*. And, second, God's laws are given for our *benefit*.

A person who accepts biblical morality is not necessarily legalistic. She or he may be, but this does not necessarily follow. Legalism is a misuse of laws. That is, the legalist keeps precepts for the wrong reasons. The Bible itself speaks against three different types of legalism.

Scripture addresses the mistaken belief that one can become acceptable to God by keeping, or trying to keep, the law. Myriads of people today believe that if they do the best they can, God is obligated to accept them at death. These people are to be commended for attempting to live a moral life, but they are mistaken. Their efforts and their accomplishments, no matter how commendable they may be, fall far short of what God requires. The Bible speaks of salvation as a "gift" (Eph. 2:8–9). This is because forgiveness is never earned, it is received. Since no one can *do* enough to please God, His requirements can only be met when we trust in the sacrifice of Christ, made on the cross (Luke 24:27, 44; 1 Cor. 15:1–5).* A major

---

*Christ's death was a ransom, paying the price of the penalty for sin (Matt. 20:28; 1 Tim. 2:6). It was threefold in scope: a reconciliation (2 Cor. 5:18–19), an atoning sacrifice (1 John 2:2), and a substitution (2 Cor. 5:21).

purpose of the law is that we might see our need of divine grace (Gal. 3:24). It is not given so that we might be challenged to earn favor (Eph. 2:9).

A second type of legalism is that which the apostle Paul treats in his letter to the Galatian church. His listeners understood clearly that forgiveness comes by faith alone, apart from works. But at the same time they believed that their spiritual growth was totally dependent on their own ability to keep some of the religious observances of the Old Testament. They were wrong. They not only did not understand that the dietary regulations of the Old Testament were now passé, but, equally serious, they were not depending on the power of the Holy Spirit. According to Scripture, the Holy Spirit indwells every Christian believer (1 Cor. 6:19). Their spiritual growth, Paul taught, was dependent on the Spirit. Paul also chides them for expecting to be perfected through their own effort, after having begun the Christian life by depending on the Spirit (Gal. 3:3).

The Pharisees represented a third type of legalism. They added their own traditions to the laws that had been given by God. Thus they became entangled in "splitting hairs," that is, making fine distinctions about points of the Old Testament law. Christ denounced them for this (Mark 7:6–8).

These ancient forms of legalism are still with us today. The problem is not the moral precepts of the Bible, but rather with misguided responses to what God has revealed.

The answer to legalism? It is to recognize our need for divine enablement to meet God's requirements. Objectively, this takes place when we see our need to accept Christ's provision for forgiveness. Subjectively, this means that we must depend on the indwelling Spirit, so that our outward obedience is combined with a proper attitude. Jesus' teaching on murder is an example of the blending of obedience and attitude. The commandment, "You shall not murder," retains its full force. But along with this Christ says that if we hate another person we are murderers in our hearts. The same is true of adultery and theft. Though outward obedience is better than disobedience, God wants outward obedience to be coupled with a corresponding inner attitude. *This* is not legalism.

Since God is the Creator and His moral revelation is based on His nature, we are assured that His precepts are for our benefit. We're all acquainted with that caricature of God as a scrooge who wants to take the fun out of life. God is pictured as one who cannot tolerate people who have a good time. But such an opinion is wide of the mark.

7. God's Moral Revelation Was Given for the Benefit of Mankind

Admittedly, God's precepts do restrict us. There are certain actions that are prohibited by the commandments. Although it may sometimes appear to us that such restrictions are unnecessary, the fact remains that God our Creator can evaluate our conduct from the perspective of eternity.

Think of the account of the fall of man in the Bible (Gen. 3). When Adam and Eve saw the fruit, it looked good to eat. It was also pleasant to the eyes, and it was indeed something to be desired if it would make one wise. They ignored God's prohibition, perhaps thinking there was nothing inherently right in commandments themselves or that it would be naïve to obey a law simply because God said so. Therefore, thinking that they had adequately evaluated the consequences, and probably having reasoned that there could be nothing wrong with food, they made an "agapeic calculus"* of sorts (as the situationist would recommend) and ate the fruit. But the results were far more disastrous than they had imagined. Why? Because a man and a woman thought that morality could be judged by the consequences, and that *they* had the ability to calculate and predict this outcome.

But because Adam and Eve were limited by time and by human knowledge, they could not predict the catastrophe that would result. Whenever we question God's moral revelation, we question His wisdom. But as the Creator, God alone can calculate eternal conse-

---

*An agapeic calculus is a calculation of the consequences of some action, using a formula in which "love" is the yardstick for judging whether or not an action should be carried out.

quences. God alone knows best because He is omniscient.

8. Any Exception to God's Revelation Must Have Biblical Sanction

In any discussion of biblical ethics, the question arises as to what kind of conduct pleases God in those special situations in which two universal moral laws appear to be in conflict.[67] For example, would it be right to tell a lie to save a life? We must, of course, be careful not to build an ethical system on such unusual cases, as, for example, Fletcher does. John Macquarrie writes, "An ethic cannot be built on exceptions. Indeed, hard cases can be recognized only because there is already a tacit assumption of norms."[68] So, although special cases must be considered and allowed for in any ethical system, they should not detract us from the clarity of biblical revelation in the moral choices that each one of us faces daily.

Any system of ethics built upon biblical absolutes will agree that in biblical ethics we are not to judge morality by calculating the consequences of an act. God has established the moral law; our responsibility is obedience. He must take care of the consequences. Daniel did what was right and God spared his life; others have been martyred for their faith. But in both of these situations the Christian believes that God is sovereign and that He can order the consequences as He wishes. We obey the rules; He keeps the score.

Let us now reconsider the case of Mrs. Bergmeier (see chapter 3) in the Russian prison camp. Was she in fact faced with the dilemma of obeying the moral law or doing what was best for all concerned? It may indeed seem so, but we must consider all of the questions that have to be answered in making a decision such as she did. Here are but some of these questions: What will the psychological consequences be for Deitrich when he discovers the circumstances of his conception? Will there be alienation between Mrs. Bergmeier and her husband and family as a result of this liaison? Finally, what about eternal consequences? The last question must be asked as well as the others because there is more to life than our temporal experiences.

We can sympathize with Mrs. Bergmeier. We might even be tempted to excuse her, arguing that what she did was understandable given the circumstances. Human sentiment, however, is not an adequate base for making reliable moral judgments. Having done what was best from God's perspective will also prove to be best for one's family and friends.

Perhaps the case of Mrs. Bergmeier can be put into perspective with another true story. During a Communist purge, a teen-age boy was being tortured in order to force his father, a minister, to commit adultery (evidently for the purpose of blackmail). The father was told that if he followed orders, his son would be released. Seeing his son being beaten, the father was about to agree when his son shouted, "Dad, don't do it! I would rather die than have a dad who is a coward and who would betray my mother."

Love does not always mean the easy path. Love does not sacrifice honor or integrity for immediate gratification, no matter how noble one's intentions. Love can wait until all the results are in.

9. "Ought" Does Not Always Imply "Can"

The eighteenth-century philosopher Immanuel Kant caused a revolution in the field of epistemology, the study of the origin and limits of human knowledge. His thought also provided the basis for an ethical theory. Kant contended that *ought* always implied *can:* whatever we ought to do, we can do.

This, however, is contrary to the biblical teaching that we do not, and cannot, live up to what we know to be right. The apostle Paul, author of many of the New Testament writings, described his own struggles in this way: "For that which I am doing, I do not understand; for I am not practicing what I would like to do, but I am doing the very thing I hate" (Rom. 7:15, NASB).

Perhaps it appears that God has deceived us. He has given us a moral standard that is beyond our ability. To give requirements that cannot be kept smacks of mockery.

There is, however, one fact we must keep in mind in all of this. Christ's death on the cross satisfied

God's requirements. Perhaps an illustration will help here.

After a man had pleaded guilty to a traffic violation, the judge announced that he would have to pay a fine. However, the moment after the judge demanded the payment, he left the bench, stood next to the defendant, and paid the fine for him! The judge, who was also the father of the defendant, handed down the sentence, but he also paid it.

So it is with God, our Creator. Our attempts at reaching His standard of righteousness are hopeless. But God identified Himself with the human race so that He could satisfy His own requirements on our behalf. Those who depend on the sacrifice of Christ are guaranteed acceptance before God.

Conclusion

A biblical approach to ethics provides a framework that is rationally consistent and that corresponds truly to our humanity, including our deepest needs. It originates with God rather than with man, and it thus provides a satisfying answer to the question, what makes an act right or wrong? The answer is: the revealed will of God found in the Bible.

Some may wish for an alternative to relativism that is less "religious" in nature. Some may wonder how we could reach traditional "Sunday" territory, especially after having discussed Douglas Templemore poisoning his "child," the *paranthropus erectus*, at the outset of this book. Such a shift is necessary because there are no other alternatives to help us find our way out of the jungles of naturalistic ethics.

The ethic we live by will be determined by our understanding of reality and by the limitations of human knowledge. If we opt for a closed system, with a naturalistic theory of origins, we are free to select from the options offered in chapters 2 through 5. If we opt for an open system where God is present, we have the additional possibility of revealed standards that transcend all human opinion—either of the one or the majority—and that may be used as a yardstick to evaluate all human behavior.

Every philosophical and ethical lens we try will

either distort or bring into focus what reality *really*
is—metaphysically, epistemologically, and ethically.
The question for every human being to answer is,
Which lens clearly depicts reality? That question must
be answered first before one can enter into meaningful
discussion about ethical systems.

Our choice of a theory of ethics, then, is not a
trivial one. My experience in counseling has convinced me that an ethical standard can mean the difference between hope and despair for the person
facing perplexing ethical choices. Those who accept
the biblical framework will be spared the arbitrary values of relativism, with its inevitable despair. Only such a
decisive moral commitment can provide hope in the
midst of the uncertainty and instability of our times.

Response

Response

Apart from very young children and the mentally deranged, no human being is amoral. Indeed, the capacity for moral thinking and moral behavior is one of the most surprising characteristics of human beings. What makes it particularly surprising to us today is the pervasive naturalism and secular humanism that form much of the backdrop of contemporary education.

MARK M. HANNA

Why should human beings raise ethical questions? How can we account for the phenomenon of moral valuation? Why do we ask what we *ought* to do; that is, why do we speak in terms of rightness or goodness, and not merely in terms of consequences? Why do we praise or blame ourselves and others for specific attitudes and actions?

Some psychotherapists observe that it is typical for human beings to use 85 percent of their psychic energy suppressing feelings of guilt. Why do we have these guilt feelings? Why are we aware that there is an unbridgeable gap between what we know we ought to be and what we are? What is the significance of the human capacity to apprehend and strive for moral ideals? And our inability to achieve them?

Naturalistic evolution does not provide adequate answers to these questions. How moral awareness could have developed out of matter—irrespective of the complexity of its organization—is an impenetrable puzzle.

Why has moral awareness appeared in human beings? It is certainly not necessary for mere survival. After all, many species of animals have not only survived without it but to this day they exhibit superior potential for viability. Those most likely to survive terrestrial catastrophes are the various kinds of insects, which make up an estimated 78 percent of all the creatures on earth. And they certainly do not display any capacity for moral judgment or moral conduct. As Erwin Lutzer rightly points out, philosophical naturalism fails both in its attempt to account for the ethical dimension and in its effort to answer crucial ethical questions.

The importance of moral experience can hardly be overestimated, for today the human race stands on the brink of self-destruction. It is not first of all technology but moral decision-making that will determine whether or not we have a future, and if so, what kind of a future it will be.

There is a fundamental difference between that which is expedient and that which is right. All attempts to erase that distinction between good and bad, right and wrong, have been signal failures. Since moral experience is universal, and since moral distinctions cannot be eradicated, Lutzer rightly focuses on the question: "What makes an action right or wrong?" Is an action morally right merely because the majority of people agree that it is? Is an action right because an individual or group has the power to compel certain actions or to punish those who do not follow their orders? Lutzer cogently argues that neither mere majority opinion nor mere might can determine what is morally right. The *ought* of morality cannot be derived from the *is* of "consensus" or the *is* of "might."

The author examines four major ethical theories. He shows that the first approach, ethical relativism, is untenable because it invariably smuggles absolutes into its perspective. For instance, in one of its forms, it teaches that the highest value is conformity to one's culture: that is, each person apparently has a *moral* obligation to abide by the consensus of his or her own culture. Yet any culture in which the majority believes that there are transcultural, universal absolutes is judged to be holding a wrong opinion by cultural relativists. Accordingly, both the cultural outsider and insider are called upon to oppose the status quo of the culture in question. Praising and blaming the actions of cultures requires an appeal, tacit or explicit, to a moral touchstone that transcends cultures.

Situation ethics does not fare any better. Its ambiguous, and virtually contentless, notion of love pre-

cludes its applicability to moral decisions. The dev-
asting criticisms that have been issued against
utilitarianism apply to this ethical perspective as well,
for it, too, explicitly states that the end justifies the
means. Such an assumption concerning human
morality reduces goodness and rightness to expe-
diency and its appeal to love as a moral absolute results in nonsense.

B. F. Skinner advocates a society built on the presuppositions of behavioristic determinism. In effect,
however, he says that it is morally right to construct
such a society and it is morally wrong to treat people
as if they were free to choose and do other than they
have. His *social ought,* therefore, is inescapably a
moral ought. In addition to taking note of this inconsistency, we should also observe that if human beings
are totally at the mercy of heredity and environment,
social oughts, no less than moral oughts, are a mockery.

The last approach to ethics treated in this book,
emotivist theories of ethics, errs in a number of ways.
The fundamental flaw, of course, is the self-defeating
nature of the principle of verifiability that underlies
such theories. Ethical categories and judgments cannot be rejected on the basis of a principle that makes
itself meaningless—meaningless in the sense that it
purports to be informative but cannot be empirically
verified.

Whether we take an inductive or hypothetico-
deductive model of scientific method, neither one can
yield an ethical theory. Every ethical proposition
transcends *de*scription with *pre*scription, and thereby
reveals the presence of a plus factor over and above
all of the empirical data of the natural sciences.

In contrast to all such theories, whether ethical or
antiethical, the surpassing value of Christian ethics is
discernible in several ways, as Lutzer explains. The
Bible, which is the source of Christian ethics, is rationally credible as the revelation of God, for its
claims are corroborated by a wide range of evidence,
from archaeology to logic. This revelation exhibits an
unmatched realism about the nature, conduct, and as-
pirations of human beings. It presents the highest

ethical standard available anywhere; for example, no illustration of moral ideals can be found to surpass the Sermon on the Mount or the "love chapter" of the Bible, 1 Corinthians 13. The Bible's integrating center is the historical person of Jesus Christ, who alone has completely exemplified the moral perfections He taught.

God's revelation alone makes sense out of the moral experience of human beings, explaining why it is that we have moral awareness (an explanation that is based on the image of God in man) and why it is that a yawning chasm exists between what we are and what we sense we should be (because sin and evil do exist in the world). In the final analysis, the Bible presents the answer to the moral failure of human beings: God's freely given forgiveness by means of the redeeming death and resurrection of Christ.

This clearly written book will help people to think through the critical issues at stake in ethical inquiry, and it will help them to realize how the biblical position alone adequately provides the rationale for and, at the same time, meets the need for ethical absolutes.

References

References

[1]William Graham Sumner, *Folkways* (Boston: Ginn and Company, 1906), p. 76.

[2]Melville J. Herskovits, *Cultural Relativism* (New York: Random House, 1973), p. 15.

[3]Ibid.

[4]Ibid., p. 56.

[5]Wayne A. Leys, *Ethics and Social Policy* (New York: Prentice-Hall, 1941), p. 184.

[6]Antony Flew, *Evolutionary Ethics* (New York: St. Martin's Press, 1968), p. 55.

[7]Ibid., pp. 57–58.

[8]Ibid., p. 60.

[9]"Save Us! Save Us!" in *Time,* 9 July 1979, p. 28.

[10]*Cultural Relativism,* p. 32.

[11]Joseph Fletcher, *Situation Ethics: The New Morality* (Philadelphia: Westminster Press, 1966), pp. 164–65.

[12]Ibid., p. 18.

[13]John A. T. Robinson, *Honest to God* (Philadelphia: Westminster Press, 1963), p. 112.

[14]*Situation Ethics,* p. 30.

[15]Gordon H. Clark, *A Christian View of Men and Things* (Grand Rapids: Wm. B. Eerdmans, 1951), p. 188.

[16]Joseph Fletcher, "What's in a Rule?: A Situationist's View," in Gene Outka and Paul Ramsey, eds., *Norm and Context in Christian Ethics* (New York: Scribners, 1968), p. 332.

[17]J. E. Barnhart, "Egoism and Altruism," *Southwestern Journal of Philosophy* 7, no. 1 (Winter 1976): 101–110.

[18]Joseph Fletcher, *Moral Responsibility* (Philadelphia: Westminster Press, 1968), p. 23.

[19]*Situation Ethics,* p. 121.

[20]Ibid., p. 55.

[21]Lawrence Richards, "To Do the Loving Thing Manward," *Action* (Spring 1968), p. 23.

[22]*Situation Ethics,* p. 39.

[23]Ibid., p. 110.

[24]Ibid., p. 115.

[25]Ibid., pp. 115–16.

[26]Paul Ramsey, *Deeds and Rules in Christian Ethics* (New York: Scribners, 1967), p. 190.

[27]*Situation Ethics,* p. 136.

[28]*Moral Responsibility*, p. 32.

[29]John Stuart Mill, *Utilitarianism* (Indianapolis: Bobbs-Merrill, 1957), chapter 2.

[30]*Moral Responsibility*, p. 32.

[31]*Situation Ethics*, p. 117.

[32]Ibid., p. 118.

[33]*Time*, 1 August 1977.

[34]Ibid., p. 54.

[35]For a complete discussion of the mind-body problem, see Arthur C. Custance, *The Mysterious Matter of Mind* (Grand Rapids: Zondervan/Probe, 1980). For a fuller discussion of human nature, see Mark P. Cosgrove, *The Essence of Human Nature* (Grand Rapids: Zondervan/Probe, 1977).

[36]Julien Offray de La Mettrie, *Man a Machine* (1747) in Norman L. Torrey, ed., *Les Philosophes* (New York: Capricorn Books, 1960), p. 177.

[37]Thomas Huxley, "Mr. Darwin's Critics," *Contemporary Review* (November, 1871), p. 464.

[38]*Time*, 1 August 1977, p. 57.

[39]B. F. Skinner, *Beyond Freedom and Dignity* (New York: Alfred A. Knopf, 1971), p. 200.

[40]Quoted in Frederick Copleston, S. J., *A History of Philosophy*, vol. 6, *Modern Philosophy: The French Enlightenment to Kant*, part 1 (Garden City, N.Y.: Doubleday & Company, 1964), p. 65.

[41]Mortimer J. Adler, *The Difference of Man and the Difference It Makes* (New York: Holt, Rinehart and Winston, 1967), p. 221.

[42]Wilder Penfield et al., *The Mystery of the Mind* (Princeton, N.J.: Princeton University Press, 1975), p. 80.

[43]David Hume, *A Treatise of Human Nature* (Oxford: The Clarendon Press, 1888), p. 468.

[44]A. J. Ayer, *Language, Truth and Logic* (New York: Dover Publications, 1952), pp. 107–8.

[45]Ibid., p. 103.

[46]Ibid., p. 112.

[47]In William K. Frankena, *Ethics* (Englewood Cliffs, N.J.: Prentice Hall, 1973), p. 106.

[48]C. L. Stevenson, "Noncognitivism and Relativism," in Paul W. Taylor, ed., *Problems of Moral Philosophy* (Belmont, Calif.: Wadsworth Publishing Co., 1978), pp. 370–82.

[49]Quoted by Francis Schaeffer in *Back to Freedom and Dignity* (Downers Grove, Ill.: InterVarsity Press, 1972), p. 13.

[50]Carl F. H. Henry, *Christian Personal Ethics* (Grand

Rapids: Wm. B. Eerdmans Publishing Co., 1957), p. 125.

[51]Stephen C. Pepper, *Ethics* (New York: Appleton-Century Crafts, 1960), p. 281.

[52]W. H. Werkmeister, *Theories of Ethics* (Lincoln, Neb.: Johnsen Publishing Co., 1961), p. 33.

[53]John Dewey, *Logic: The Theory of Inquiry* (New York: H. Holt and Company, 1938), p. 216.

[54]*Situation Ethics*, pp. 43–44.

[55]Ibid., p. 39.

[56]*Moral Responsibility*, p. 137.

[57]*Situation Ethics*, p. 42.

[58]Ibid., p. 129.

[59]Ibid.

[60]Gordon H. Clark, s.v. "Humanism," in Carl F. H. Henry, ed., *Baker's Dictionary of Christian Ethics* (Grand Rapids: Baker Book House, 1973).

[61]For a full discussion of the deity and authority of Jesus Christ, see Jon. A Buell and O. Quentin Hyder, *Jesus: God, Ghost or Guru?* (Grand Rapids: Zondervan/Probe, 1978).

[62]*Situation Ethics*, p. 139.

[63]Ibid., p. 97.

[64]Joseph Fletcher and John Warwick Montgomery, *Situation Ethics: True or False?* (Minneapolis, Minn.: Bethany Fellowship, 1972), p. 55.

[65]*Situation Ethics*, p. 126.

[66]Peter Abelard, *Abailard's Ethics* (Oxford: Basil Blackwell, 1935), p. 29.

[67]For a discussion of various biblical approaches to moral conflicts, see Norman Geisler, *Ethical Alternatives and Issues* (Grand Rapids: Zondervan, 1971).

[68]John Macquarrie, *Three Issues in Ethics* (New York: Harper & Row, 1970), pp. 39–40.

For Further Reading

For Further Reading

Adler, Mortimer J. **The Difference of Man and the Difference It Makes.** New York: Holt, Rinehart and Winston, 1967.

In this volume, Adler constructs a logic for determining how man is unlike everything else. He then applies this to various philosophical and scientific theories and concludes that, on the evidence we have up to now, man differs in kind from all other things, rather than merely by degree.

Clark, Gordon H. **Religion, Reason and Revelation.** Nutley, New Jersey: The Craig Press, 1961.

This Christian philosopher examines the relationships between philosophy (reason), religion (Christianity), and biblical revelation. He finds that the Bible accurately and authoritatively presents Christianity as a satisfying philosophical system. He also demonstrates how the Christian view sets forth a system of ethics that conforms to reality and, therefore, is practical.

Clark, Gordon H. **Thales to Dewey.** Boston: Houghton Mifflin Company, 1957.

Clark presents a thorough history of philosophy in this volume. He provides a chronicle of the relationship of theories of knowledge (epistemology) to other aspects of philosophy (including ethics).

Erickson, Millard J. **Relativism in Contemporary Christian Ethics.** Grand Rapids: Baker Book House, 1974.

A contemporary Christian theologian examines the ethical concerns of our day and takes a critical stand against various forms of relativism. Although it is addressed primarily to a Christian audience, this book may also be helpful to unbelievers.

Frankena, William K. **Ethics.** 2nd ed. Englewood Cliffs, New Jersey: Prentice-Hall, 1973.

An excellent introduction to the subject of ethics, this vol- 107 *ume is written for the undergraduate philosophy student. Part of the "Foundations of Philosophy" series.*

Fletcher, Joseph. **Situation Ethics: The New Morality.** Philadelphia: Westminster Press, 1966.

This is the classic presentation of the "new morality," by its chief proponent. The author defends what he claims is a Christian view of relativism.

Geisler, Norman. **Ethics: Alternatives and Issues.** Grand Rapids: Zondervan Publishing House, 1971.

This book is written from a decidedly evangelical perspective. Geisler gives an excellent discussion of various biblical approaches to moral conflicts.

Henry, Carl F. H., ed. **Baker's Dictionary of Christian Ethics.** Grand Rapids: Baker Book House, 1973.

A look at nearly every ethical system, problem, and issue by a wide range of evangelical scholars. This work is invaluable for the student who wishes to read a brief biblical evaluation of many of the issues and moral conflict situations one may face both in college life and in the classroom.

Henry, Carl F. H. **Christian Personal Ethics.** Grand Rapids: Wm. B. Eerdmans Publishing Co., 1957.

The most thorough defense of the evangelical Christian ethical system written by any contemporary theologian.

Herskovits, Melville J. **Cultural Relativism.** New York: Random House, 1973.

The classic presentation of the ethical system that proclaims, "Culture determines what is right."

Mill, John Stuart. **Utilitarianism.** Indianapolis: Bobbs-Merrill, 1957.

This is a standard text for the utilitarian ethical system. Mill defends especially qualitative utilitarianism.

Murray, John. **Principles of Conduct.** Grand Rapids: Wm. B. Eerdmans Publishing Co., 1957.

This work is based on a series of lectures presented by Professor Murray at Fuller Theological Seminary, and it is addressed specifically to a Christian audience. He outlines biblical aspects of ethics, from a Reformed view.

Outka, Gene, and Ramsey, Paul, eds. **Norm and Context in Christian Ethics.** New York: Scribners, 1968.

A view of Christian ethics from the neo-orthodox and neo-evangelical standpoints.

Schaeffer, Francis A. **Back to Freedom and Dignity.** Downers Grove: InterVarsity Press, 1972.

This is a short book, dealing with some current scientific theories that seek to dehumanize man. There is an excellent discussion of the ramifications of accepting chemical evolution and psychological determinism.

Schaeffer, Francis A., and Koop, C. Everett. **Whatever Happened to the Human Race?** Old Tappan, New Jersey: Fleming H. Revell Co., 1979.

Exploring an explosive issue, abortion, the authors expose the modern trends toward manipulation of human rights through bio-medical means (abortion, euthanasia, and infanticide). They view this as evidence of a loss of human dignity and a decreasing appreciation for ethical values in Western culture. They point to relativistic ethics as a major cause of this erosion and chart a course for a return to a biblical base for moral values. Thus, they believe, will human dignity and rights be restored.

Skinner, B. F. **Beyond Freedom and Dignity.** New York: Alfred A. Knopf, 1971.

The standard—and controversial—work outlining human behavior from the standpoint of scientific materialism, based upon evolutionary presuppositions. Skinner sees human beings as animals that have ended a high stage of evolution and whose ethics are based solely on a response to the conditioning factors in their environment.

Stevenson, Charles L. **Ethics and Language.** New Haven, Connecticut: Yale University Press, 1945.

A normative text on emotivist ethics.

Wilson, Edward O. **On Human Nature.** Cambridge, Massachusetts: Harvard University Press, 1978.

This volume examines the impact on the social sciences and humanities of an evolutionary explanation of human behavior. The follow-up to the author's previous work, **Sociobiology: The New Synthesis,** *it explores the extension of population biology and evolutionary theory to human social organization. Like Skinner, Wilson speaks from the point of view of the scientific materialist.*

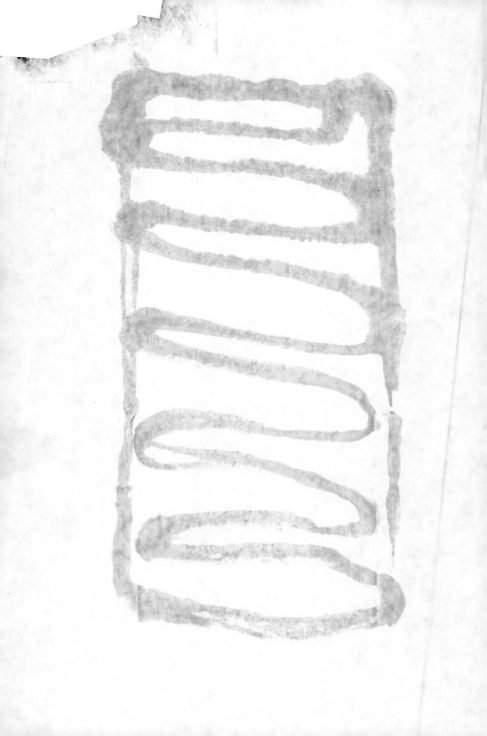